The Essential Coaching Book

The Essential Coaching Book

Secrets to a Winning Life
from the Professional and Personal Coaches
of the United Coaching Associates

United Coaching Associates, Inc.

iUniverse, Inc.
New York   Lincoln   Shanghai

The Essential Coaching Book
Secrets to a Winning Life from the Professional and Personal Coaches
of the United Coaching Associates

iUniverse, Inc.

For information address:
iUniverse, Inc.
2021 Pine Lake Road, Suite 100
Lincoln, NE 68512
www.iuniverse.com

ISBN: 0-595-33048-7

Printed in the United States of America

The Essential Coaching Book would not be possible without the hard work and dedication of the business and life coaches of the United Coaching Associates, Inc. Their willingness to pursue new challenges and take risks on a consistent basis makes them the incredible coaches they are today.

United Coaching Associates, Inc. of Long Island, NY is an affiliate of two premier training institutions for professional coaches, Coach U (Steamboat Springs, CO at http://www.coachu.com) and CoachVille (http://www.coachville.com). We owe our existence as a membership group to these two organizations, devoted to the professional and ethical practice of the profession called 'coaching'. They were both founded by one remarkable dynamo of creativity and productivity that literally created this field some 20 years ago. Thomas Leonard (www.thomasleonard.com) passed away in 2003 having launched tens of thousands of individuals into their next profession and life. We thank Thomas. He put a name to a series of life affirming techniques for those seeking the richness of all the unique qualities, values, dreams and priorities they possess. He imbued it with ethics, perspective, tools, content, required training and made it into a worldwide phenomenon.

Deborah Brown-Volkman, President; Andrea Feinberg, Vice President; United Coaching Associates, Inc.

Contents

Introduction

You are about to enter the world of personal transformation. Each chapter in this book represents an opportunity, yours to select, that will lead you towards a happier and more productive life. Included are chapters on how to set your vision with concrete steps to get you there, whether your vision is guiding you towards romance, career enhancement, inner growth, a well-run business, physical health or a means to plan and enjoy the rest of your life.

This book has been written by 15 authors. Each is a member coach of United Coaching Associates, Inc. The United Coaching Associates, Inc., created in October 2001, offers on-going training and development for coaches as well as a resource for those who are looking for the perfect business or personal coach. Each coach is knowledgeable and passionate about their area of expertise, shared within these pages.

This book was written as a collaborative effort so you could receive a variety of perspectives that will lead to the same goal—a satisfying, successful life for you, on your own terms, no matter how you define "a winning life," having everything you want and more. Throughout this book, we'll each be your partner as you work through the suggestions and exercises that resonate with you. Additionally, at the end of this book you'll find resources to continue the exploration of subjects most meaningful for you.

We know getting there is not always easy, but it is worth the trip. We are happy you chose to take this journey with us.

What Is Coaching?

This book provides a perfect opportunity to discover and explore what it would be like to have a coach in your life or business. Coaches use a pretty big tool kit to help clients get from where they are today to where they'd like to be—tomorrow, next year and in years to come. Whether you've wanted some focused support to enhance work, parenting, your business, a personal relationship, health, time management or discovering your true life's purpose, professional coaches are the ideal partners to assist you.

In helping clients clarify and fulfill their goals, we incorporate such tools as listening, focused questioning, empowering, challenging, advising, making distinctions and supporting. We have no agenda, no guideline to direct you other than the values, priorities and needs you express as personally meaningful.

Many people are often confused about the distinctions between coaching and other disciplines. Here are some examples:

Let's say you're in business and you've come to a crossroads where things have stopped working and growing as they have in the past or as you'd expect, considering the effort you're expending. You might want to hire a consultant to assess what's happening, lay out what needs to be done, or even execute that plan for you. On the other hand, if you feel that you'd like to learn new skills and techniques so you can respond to similar situations in the future with an ability to prioritize, determine doable goals, and a timeline to accomplish them, a coach may be your next step.

Maybe you're in a career that has stopped intriguing you with its content and opportunity. If you want someone to review other options with, someone to tell you what training you need, what you can expect to make and put you in touch with possible employers, hire a career counselor. However, if you think it's time to re-evaluate the priorities in your life, the kind of people with whom you interact, the skills and strengths you want to employ and the passion you'd like to express, a coach may be your next step.

If you've become depressed and your behavior and feelings are preventing you from leading a productive life, a therapist may be a better choice. However, if you're functioning at a perfectly appropriate level of behavior yet feel something important is missing from your life, a sense of true purpose and a way to express that, a coach may be your next step.

With coaching, it's all about support and accountability. We're very big on encouraging you to take actions in your dreams, visions, or goals. We all know how important it is to identify what we most want to accomplish, yet taking the first step, and then the next one, until we get a momentum going, is very hard. And that's the perfect reason to engage a coach. You receive professional, supportive assistance in moving forward now, with a roadmap to get you there.

Whether you are looking for a coach, or are a coach who wants to connect with other coaches, you have a home with us. You are welcome to contact any of us, through our **Find A Coach Page** at http://www.unitedcoachingassociates.com/findacoach.html or our home page at http://www.unitedcoachingassociates.com You can also e-mail us at uca@unitedcoachingassociates.com We'd love to hear how you are doing and welcome your feedback and suggestions we can add to our tool box.

Chapter One:
Starting The Journey

The Power of Intentions
Written By Leslie K. Malin

There is an old saying and it goes like this, "You'll never know when you arrive at your destination unless you set your course." When we become clear on the course we are charting, it profoundly forms, shapes, and directs our activity; sometimes drawing us into exciting currents we never anticipated. Charting a course can trigger an equally powerful early warning system that jolts us when we are waffling or off course.

But what is the real nature of Intention in setting your course?

I used to think that to live with intention was to set goals, conceptualize tangible specific and materially oriented outcomes, measure out what I should accomplish to meet those goals within specific time frames and proceed in a somewhat mechanistic manner steadily towards their achievement.

That understanding doesn't work for me anymore.

Those things I mentioned are important and steadying and they reside in the realm of goal accomplishment, endings, and the finite. Intention, for me, has become a much bigger, more encompassing and spiritually formed force. Intention has turned into a continuous river-like current, a source of courage, strength, clarity and hope—a divining rod for my entire life.

As I sat down to write this chapter, I was struck by how much my own under-standing of this word has morphed and evolved over time. I have decided to relate experience, hopes and aspirations, failures and missteps that I have encountered along the way so that I may offer you my current understanding, not only of what Intention and Intentionality are, but more fundamentally, why they are so important, especially at this juncture of our lives and the state of the world.

The word *intend* is a verb designating action and movement. It derives from the words *to aim at* and *to stretch*. It encompasses having a purpose or a plan, as well as to mean how something should be used or designed and to signify purpose.

The word *intent* is an adjective, thus a descriptor indicating a mind firmly fixed, engrossed and strongly resolved. In the law, the word carries enormous significance as it relates to culpability or, as I see it, "ownership" of a force of energy in mind or in action, the nature of one's intent reflecting one's conscious state of mind and planning.

And, *intention* is a noun—the naming of something. It reflects the determination to do a specified thing or act. A determination, I believe, is a commitment and often a prayer.

Intentions are powerful things that are directional, volitional, conscious, and charged with energy. With clear intention we can piggyback the energy of the universe, we can fuel our dreams, we can gather allies and supporters, and we can marshal our resources. Further, I believe that all intentions begin as prayer for whatever we believe is within our higher good. Now, you may object, "What of the intention of a terrorist? Is that in the higher good? Well, I'm afraid to acknowledge it, but to them it is. They don't perceive their intentions as acts of evil but rather acts of redemption and salvation.

The lesson is to be careful what you intend towards. What you manifest can become much larger and more forceful than anything you dreamt possible and you may not be ready for the outcomes. If you haven't built a strong enough foundation, or have the proper support team, or have the financial and other resources in place, you can careen wildly into outer space like a psychotic rocket, filled with fuel and strength but misguided and off course. And the passengers on this rocket can be your hope, courage and self-confidence. After such a misguided adventure some people can become too frightened to fuel up again, preferring to stay "safe," earth-bound and near-sighted.

I discovered that my original definition of intention was too small and confined when I realized that my anxiety about unpredictability was keeping me tethered to perceived "safety"; I had exchanged winged feet for concrete boots. With my formula for Intention equaling pragmatic, definable action-steps, I deluded myself into believing that I already knew the "right" direction for my energies, that I had the map and that I just had to stay on the right highway. No detours for me, I thought, no exploring those tantalizing byways. "Do it by the book, just stay focused," I would tell myself.

Guess what? I tried that. Tried that for a long while and gradually I came to understand that by being so linear and intense I had missed the bigger picture. I was pursuing the outlines of my vision and that even when I achieved them, my satisfaction turned out to be less than desired or fleeting at best. I was left holding something that possessed a lack of deeper meaning, a confusing diminution of my vision, an "OK'ness" without greatness. After a while, I had to accept that I was operating on a playing field too small for my soul.

So, now what?

I began another phase of my journey. I had to set out from the known harbor again. I had to discover a new beginning in the middle of my life. And that new beginning demanded that I let go of outcomes; humble myself in the face of life's unpredictability and find faith that the journey would be its own reward.

And here's where a new vision of Intention began to form. Since I had so rudely discovered that my very Western, aggressive accomplishment of goals and objectives was not enough to fill me, I had to redefine the journey. Please understand, you need to stay focused on where you want to go, but first you need to find something overarching, bigger than yourself, more expansive, more creative, more aligned to what you value and more connected to energies that you may intuit but can't necessarily prove. And, that bigger thing is the Field of Intention.

Why is this so important? Because, hopes can be dashed; businesses can go into ruin for uncontrollable reasons; relationships once sparkling can dim; careers can become derailed; and our efforts may be rejected once, twice and perhaps a hundred times.

What then is to keep you going? What will feed you for the next foray? How can you avoid collapse in the face of on going uncertainty? The answer is in the power of Intention.

And, how do you begin to design this intention? You take the first steps out in faith. You have to embrace that you are on the road and don't know what you will meet within the next moment. All you can depend upon is this very moment. The moment a second before has already past and the future is a second and ahead around a curve. What you are left with then is your intention of stepping firmly into this very moment and fully occupying it, And, hope that as you take the next steps, you will learn more of what is truly important to you and you will hold fast to what is essential and trust that what you will create will be everlasting because it resides within you, it belongs to you and defines you.

But you won't discover those forces until you find the courage to start the journey.

You are the center of your universe—this isn't selfishness, self-centeredness or false pride, this is truth. We are our own universe and who we are is in relationship to all the other universes we encounter. I discovered that I could only define my landscape, discover my deepest oceans, climb my most challenging mountains by starting the journey in the valley. A quote I once found says it nicely, "Travelers, there is no path, paths are made by walking."

Our intentions, I believe must start from the inside out. Many of us have been raised to believe that we can create our insides, our being, our success, our riches, and our security by conquering the outside world through the ferocity of willful intentions and then our insides will reflect our accomplishment and our glory. So believing, some warrior spirits venture forth armed to the teeth with indomitable intentions. Others who believe the same myth judge themselves too weak and insignificant for the task and never leave a small, confined space, intending only to stay safe; to stay under the radar where they fervently pray that the pain and confusion of life can't find them.

What does it mean to have Intention? It means that we have to start somewhere. It doesn't necessarily mean that we know exactly where we want to land, When Itzak Perleman, the great violinist first took hand to strings and bow he didn't have the intention of playing at Carnegie Hall (that came later, I am sure). First, he wanted to create sound. Watch any young child beat a drum, blow a kazoo, or sing silly sounds and they are totally involved in what they are creating. Being a professional musician is not their intention. Making sound and thereby mimicking the world around them that is full of magnificent sound *is* their intention. That *aim*, that *stretch* is complete and realizable unto itself. The joy derived is unparalleled. I remember when Avery, my first grandson was less than 2 years old and was obsessed with the guitar. Everything within his reach he transformed into a guitar—a box, a piece of paper in the shape of a fish, a piece of cardboard we shaped into a guitar with yarn for strings—all were equal in delight and all, for him, capable of making music-in fact, he often preferred these facsimiles to the real thing. The music didn't need to be on a page, charted by notes or even audible. The music was already heard because it was resident in his heart. It was created out of his Intention. His determination made it so, while the world of reality couldn't hear a note he played.

And while he was playing each guitar within his imagination he was connected by pure joy to the source of his imagination and to the very heart of his creativity. Most of us lose that purity of intent as we get older. We get "real" which means that we shrink. We get frightened of appearing foolish, of doing something "wrong," of being laughable.

Our willful intention becomes either fixated on the attainment of specific outcomes—I will get an A on that math test, I will run that race or we shrivel up and give up. I am not discarding the power of directing energy towards a goal—but too often I have seen that when intention becomes all goal oriented it can become starved of what will provide joy and self-worth and the attainment of the very goal one sought, turns into bitter ashes. How else to understand sport superstars who self-destruct despite multi-million dollar contracts and arriving in the major leagues? Or pop-stars and movie icons who admit to debilitating drug abuse and out of control lives?

To me, it's no longer cause for surprise or shock—it is painfully predictable.

When the object of our desire does not encompass the intention to be bigger than our desires we crash and burn. If we haven't divined our true north, our soul's desire, that which is about us always, we lose our way and all the will and force in our beings can't save us. Developing guiding Intention is no easy task. Difficult to come by and often showing up later in our lives, it takes time to maturate and manifest. We humans seem to be creatures that need to do fire walks before we find paths fit for walking.

And while I don't believe lives can become tempered into steel without pain, confusion and challenge, I think there are lighthouses to guide us in finding protection from the storm; helping us to travel in the direction of something large and wonder-filled. On my journey, my true intentions have slowly let themselves be seen and then named. In their naming they have become my North Star, telling me when I am moving closer to "home" or deviating from and being pulled into deep space.

My intentions are not focused on getting the next project, or sealing a deal, or making X amount of money, although those goals can certainly focus my energies. My intentions are all about <u>Who</u> I want to be in the world and how I believe such a person acts, thinks, contributes, decides and declines.

<u>Who</u> I want to be is not <u>What</u> I want to be. <u>What</u> is the object and <u>Who</u> is the subjective center.

As the <u>Who</u> has emerged from behind the clouds the <u>What</u> is also appearing increasingly refined and targeted.

Some of my intentions as they are becoming more fully realized (Note: this is not equal to being accomplished) are:

- Who I intend strives for authenticity and integrity.
- Who I intend is willing to show up and be present in my life, in my family and in my community.
- Who I intend is focused on abundance rather than scarcity.
- Who I intend yearns for my own happiness and the happiness of others.
- Who I intend is Self-full in order to be giving and freely loving to others.
- Who I intend does not have to do life all alone.
- Who I intend is creative and exploratory
- Who I intend is full hearted.
- Who I intend knows that the beauty of what I love is what I do.
- Who I intend is constantly evolving.

With these as my Intentions I can measure every endeavor, every action, every relationship and every commitment. My Intentions are a *stretch*. They serve as my trajectory, determining where I take aim. They are monumental and yet attainable in the small and everyday. They point me in the direction of the Promised Land, yet as Rabbi Irwin Kula (www.simplewisdom.com) has so wisely perceived, the Promised Land is always promised—it is always beyond our reach but its promise can inspire and lead us through a wilderness towards a land of milk and honey.

As I have focused inside rather than without, the stuff of the outside has become more fully realized and more fully joy filled, exciting and inspiring, I now consciously make choices based on how they align with my Intentions. I work with clients, peers and projects that will assist me in fulfilling my Intentions because they are aligned with them and they want to fulfill like ones of their own. And, these fellow travelers are showing up more frequently because I am more attractive to them.

As we become more authentic we become more attractive—we pull that which empowers us towards ourselves. We become magnets for our higher good and theirs as well. I was recently sent the URL of a website that sends daily messages of attraction (www.perfectcustomers.com) created by Stacey Hall and Jan Brogniez. Attracting is different than Pushing. Attracting operates from the Inside Out. What we intend for ourselves becomes synonymous with Who we are becoming. As we refine our Being we tap into powerful energy that operates like a magnet in pulling what is aligned with us to us.

Here's a recent message:

"We are more attractive when we are playing with possibility."

"Today's tip is quick and effective. It's, "There is a real possibility that….""

Stacey shares "there was a period of time in my twenties when I did not have a positive attitude about the work I was doing and the people I was doing it with. The world looked dark to me and it was hard for me to believe that it could ever get any better. I consulted a coach, who gave me a mind tool that made all the difference in the world.

My coach asked me to let my mind consider that anything is always possible (even if it does not seem likely or probable).

And, he explained that once my mind was open to possibility, then new solutions and ways of seeing the world would be available to me.

From that day forth, whenever I found myself thinking that something was NOT going to go the way I wanted it to. I replaced that negative thought with: 'There is a real possibility that I can have.'

It didn't happen overnight…it took a few weeks of constant practice and eventually it did become an automatic thought pattern. Saying, 'There is a real possibility that I can have…' was the perfect tool to open my mind—and which led to many wonderful changes in my life."

Is there a situation in your business or life that appears it is not going the way you want it to go?

If so, we invite you to practice by saying, "There is a real possibility that I can have..."

The underlying power here is the change of orientation. It is not just changing a negative expectation into a positive one, Stacey, with the suggestion of her coach, changed her Intentionality. She became a person whose Intention is to be a person who sees possibility. Regardless of where those possibilities may arise, be it in her work, her relationships and//or personal life. She has shifted to connecting to the energy of possibility which is without limit.

Intentions Must Be Linked With What You Value

What you value must not just apply to how you think others should be or what you want from them. They must be essential to <u>who you want to be and how you want to live your life</u>. Remember, Intentions are a stretch; they are where you want to aim. Interestingly, we often find these Intentions within the center of that which feels most unsettling or troubling.

Beginning the Search for Intention:

Here are some suggestions that you can use to define your Intentions and to make them actionable in your life:

1. What thoughts or feelings about yourself or what you are doing most trouble you? For example, "I am not performing at my best...," Maybe they'll find out that I'm really not so..."

    Please sit down and write without stopping all the negative thoughts you have about yourself, your actions, your abilities, your fears and more. Don't lift your hand from the paper; don't stop yourself by worrying about spelling, grammar or, worse, who else may see this! I suggest writing with a fast moving pen and paper rather than a computer. I have found that the connection of mind with pen in hand is very powerful and real.

2. Put this list away for a day or two and then revisit. Now, reread what you have written. Take different colored highlighters and group the statements that you think go together by color. You will probably discover that there are several different themes. Write them down and place the representative statements below them:

Example:

Theme 1:   I am not good at my work.
Statements: I don't know enough
                     I am not careful
                     I am not respected
                     My boss is dissatisfied with my work

Sometimes, even though it's painful to admit, the source of our self-accusatory statements are not mere reflections of poor self-esteem, but are true manifestations of our actions, thoughts, and behaviors. This awareness is not to be a cause for self-recrimination and shame. Honest, dispassionate self-appraisal is the most crucial first step, not a cause to turn away. Until we are honest with ourselves, our efforts will turn up empty.

Find that some of those statements are true? Check off which ones are true and list them.

3. Next, write down next to the true statements what you could do to change that statement and What's In It for You to Do It.

Example:

Statement	What Can I Do About This	What's In It For Me?
I don't know enough	Take classes; ask for help, study	More success, less fear, less avoidance

4. What over-arching Intention could you aim for that would guide you in learning and knowing enough (and not just at work). Write them down, study them and refine them.

Example:

I intend to be a continuous learner
I intend to use fear to empower and strengthen me
I intend to be a smart, capable person who attracts other smart and capable people.

Notice that specific goals and actions can be developed out of these larger intentions. We can measure the appropriateness of our goals, action or opportunities by seeing if they bring us closer to realizing our intentions or further away.

5. Where we have resistance to actualizing our intentions is where we need to listen to our fears and face them. Learning to live by Intentions is learning to live fearlessly—not incautiously.

Example:

Intention: I surround myself with smart and capable people
Fears: My family or friends will get angry at me. I will be accused of being a social climber. Why would smart and capable people want to have anything to do with me? I'll be ridiculed and abandoned.

6. Now take one fear or anxiety at a time and tackle it.

How real is this?
What proves to me that this is true?
If it is true, is it important enough for me to do something about it?
What am I willing to risk to move closer to my Intention?
Now that I have created my Intention how will I feel if I give up on it?

7. Finally decide if this Intention is worth striving for.

Here are some other questions to consider on your way to Living with Intention:

1. If your Intentions become about Being rather than Doing what do you think the difference might be in your life?
2. How are Intentions and Goals different?

3. How might an emphasis on "Being" change your relationship to outcomes? Would your sense of well-being rest on the outcomes of your effort? If the actual outcome fell short of your desired outcome, could you still feel successful?
4. If your Intentions become your guide how might that change the nature of your work, relationships, life?
5. What would tell you if have deviated from your Intentions? What symptoms might occur? What concerns, fears or feelings might emerge? You don't need to do this alone. No one does. That's the most important piece of advice I can give you.

I am not suggesting that connecting to your Intentions is easy. How can you keep going when things get rough, confusing or painful?

Here are some suggestions for keeping on track:

1. Form an oversight committee. Find a small group of people who you respect and who appear to be striving to live bigger themselves and tell them what you are working on. Tell them why it's important to you. Ask them what they have done, what's worked or hasn't for them. They aren't there to tell you what to do. They aren't there to be critical and fault finding. They are chosen because they can be cheerleaders, have walked this road themselves, and are genuinely supportive of your growth.

2. Have some friends who want to work on Living from Intention in their lives. Meet together on a regular basis. Hire a facilitator or coach who will work with your group. Assign homework, share challenges, and learn from each other.

Don't think you have such people in your life yet? That's OK. Here are other things you can do:

1. Get a great coach; the suggestions and exercises here are good examples of what you'll work on with your coach.
2. Join a group of people seeking similar things
3. Take classes, workshops and seminars, or teleclasses. There are terrific offerings, many for free or very affordable all over the country like Omega, the Learning Annex, Adult Education, Coaching websites, Teleclasses.
4. Invest in yourself.

5. Go to the library or local bookstore and scan the shelves. I love to let books "talk to me." I buy and read what seems to call to me, even if I don't know why.

6. Go online to www.barnesandnoble.com and sign up for their online classes from published authors.

7. Sign up for daily tips and monthly ezines from a wide variety of sites which appeal to you.

8. Search the web—it's staggering what's available there.

9. Discover the power of journaling. Many years ago I discovered *The Artist's Way* by Julia Cameron, a truly transformative book. In it she describes what she calls Morning page. Each morning wake up and write down with pen and paper the first things that come into your mind—you can whine, complain, write to-do lists, rant and rave because you don't know what to write—it doesn't matter. It's a brain drain and it clears you before you begin the day. Spelling doesn't matter. Grammar doesn't matter. Being articulate and literary doesn't matter. All that matters is showing up.

   And after you show up you must write three handwritten pages. Yes, three. More is OK, but never less. Why three you ask? Because it has been proven to me that after one and a half pages something magical starts to happen and we approach bedrock—the real stuff begins to emerge. Now, you can rip it up immediately after writing it (I was terrified for the first few months that my children would find it and read it!! Then, I realized that I was afraid of what I was going to write, what I was going to find out.) And, if you keep it, don't re-read it for at least three months. And when you do re-read it, you will be shocked by how much things have shifted.

Remember, when you approach Intentions from this perspective everything in your life is touched. Your personal life is not split off from your work life. You are not some puzzle with missing pieces—you are made of whole cloth and it is all beautiful. Even though our lives are never finished works of art, they are nonetheless art from the very beginning. When we connect with the bigger forces we connect with others, we are not alone and we can tap into energies heretofore unknown. We are as big as our Intentions and more powerful than we could have ever imagined.

Setting Your Intentions
Written By Lynn B. Engeholm

"Intention is one of the most powerful forces in life. Without it we can sometimes stray without meaning or direction in our lives. But with it, all the forces of the universe can align to make even the most impossible, possible."—Marcia Wieder, America's Dream Coach

When we set an intention we are beginning our own personal process for planning future direction, purpose, and accomplishments. We are taking control of our life and stating what we want for ourselves. Intentions can be set for all areas of our life; Personal, Professional, Health, Relationships, Financial, and Fun. The power in an intention is when we communicate our intention to others. We can then be supported and held accountable for honoring our intention and doing what we say we intend to do.

I have found that intentions are an effective way to set direction for my personal development. Intentions stretch me to try something new, take a risk, go beyond the status quo, or play a bigger game. The starting point for setting an intention is knowing what I want and being able to ask for it. Clarity is important in setting an intention. I must admit that there have been times when my intentions have been vague. It is appropriate to have vague intentions when you are in the early, creative, or imaginative phase of your plan. For example, it is my intention to create space for my imagination to explore creative outlets. At this stage I want to keep all my options open and explore everything before I finalize my plan. I do caution you that remaining vague for extended periods of time can sabotage or lead to confusion, inertia, and stagnation. Success will be limited by vague intentions. Clarity in our intentions allows us to take action quickly and realize our plan.

What is the difference between defining an intention and goal setting? An intention has to do with who you are and what you want for yourself. An intention is a statement of your being. It comes from the heart. A goal has to do with what you want to achieve within a specific timeframe. Goals can be set based on an intention. A SMART goal is Specific, Measurable, Achievable or Action-oriented, Realistic, and Time bound. For example, my goal is to have a small greenhouse built in my backyard by the end of the year. It is my intention to enjoy this process. The goal will result in a completed greenhouse by the end of the year. My intention will support me in accomplishing the goal. When there is a problem, which is inevitable, my intention will allow me to continue to enjoy the process and look forward to the completed greenhouse. I will not be caught up in crisis. My intention will allow me to continue with the goal or adjust it based on new or additional information.

There is a difference between having a positive attitude and setting an intention. A positive attitude means that you are able to find the best in all situations. An intention is how you want your reality to be. An intention is from the heart and supports how you present yourself in any situation.

Here are some suggestions on when to set an intention:

1. Before you go to sleep, you can intend to remember your dreams or intend to have a restful sleep.
2. Before you get out of bed, you can intend to have a fabulous day.
3. Before you eat breakfast, you can intend to taste and enjoy it.
4. Before you leave the house, you can intend to have a heartfelt moment with your family or friends.
5. Before you start your car, you can intend to have a safe ride, or intend to find a parking space close to your store of choice at the mall.
6. Before you enter your workplace, you can intend to learn something new or be of help to someone.
7. Before you enter the house after a day at work, you can intend to be present mentally as well as physically to your spouse, children, roommate, or yourself.

Setting your intentions may or may not be easy for you. It takes determination and a personal willingness to do whatever it takes to honor your intention with action. There will be times when your commitment to your intention will be tested. The good news is that holding your intention allows you to get what you want with far less effort than you would have expected.

I recently attended a week long workshop where each attendee was asked to have an intention concerning the workshop. Each of us took time to write out our intention for the week. My statement of intention was: I intend to create a statement of my life's purpose and express it with joy and ease by the end of the week. Other attendees expressed their intention regarding what they wanted to get during the week. For example: I intend to have fun, or I intend to be present and laugh, or I intend to meet new people. Half way through the workshop I created my life purpose statement and was able to express it to the group with joy and ease. I then set a new intention for the workshop which was to take risks and have fun. That intention certainly created a new perspective for me. I challenged myself to grow and have fun while doing it. For me that was very scary, yet powerful, and it allowed me to create an unforgettable workshop experience.

The New Year is a perfect time to set new intentions for all areas of your life (Personal, Professional, Health, Relationships, Financial, and Fun). This is a tradition for me as it is for many. I start the year with my intentions drawn like a road map and am prepared to speed down the highway toward my vision. As the year draws to a close and I look back over my year's journey, I get frustrated with the times I was detoured or had to yield to another or was halted in my progress. What happened to that initial energy and desire? How did I get side-tracked during the year? How can I get back on track? Has this happened to you, too? Here are some suggestions to move you in the right direction.

Use the following to set your intentions for the year ahead.

1. Choose intentions that you really want to achieve during the year.

2. Write your intentions down and keep them visible so you see them everyday. Start your intention statement with the word "I" and use the present tense. For example: I intend to be present in all conversations that I have with my family or friends.

3. Tell friends, family, and colleagues about your intentions for the year. Who will you tell?

4. Take action on your intentions every day. What actions will you take for each of your intentions?

5. Choose your ultimate reward for achieving your plan. Write it down and keep it visible along with your intentions.

6. Celebrate your accomplishments each day! Write down ways you are going to celebrate your accomplishments.

Now set an intention for the week ahead.

1. What do you want to create in your life today? Look at all areas of your life; Personal, Professional, Health, Relationships, Financial, and Fun. For example, I want to create a space in my home where I can have some quiet time to read and listen to music.

2. What is something that you intend to do as a result of your answers to #1? For example, I will create 30 minutes a day for me to do as I wish.

3. What is your intention for what you want to accomplish this week? For example, I will clear an area in the guest bedroom for a rocking chair and a CD player.

4. How will you keep your intention alive each day? For example, I will write my intention on a 3x5 card and post it on the refrigerator, and/or I will state my intention each morning as I get out of bed.

5. Who are you going to communicate your intention to? For example, I will communicate my intention to my family and friends.

In summary, intentions are powerful. They are as powerful as the action you put into them. Think of a balloon being your intention and your resulting actions as the helium you put into the balloon. The more helium you put into the balloon the higher and longer your balloon can fly. Focused action will let you know just how much helium to put into your intention balloon to reach success.

The Ten Steps of Intention
Written By: Paula Giambalvo Rosario

So what do you want to be when you grow up? What a great question. Do you remember being asked this when you were a kid? Did you want to be a teacher, a dancer or an artist? And what happened to that dream, that wish, that intention? Did you follow it? Does it still wait to be fulfilled?

Something magical happens when we go to *that place*. You know *that place*. It's where you suspend judgment, chase away the how-am-I-going-to-get-it-done roadblocks and eliminate the have-to-do-list of obligations. It's where all that is possible exists in blissful surrender.

When we were children this was the Shangri-La of our existence. With wide-eyed excitement it was a very likely place to be. Our thoughts, wishes and intentions came to life in the world of pretend. We'd daydream and become our hearts' desires. It was sheer excitement and possibility. The outside world hadn't taught us yet how to look for reasons that would keep us from what would be our destiny.

The Grand Giraffe

I can vividly recall what seemed an enchanted event when I was seven. Our school was having a carnival and the day before it was to start our teacher, Sister Michelle, took the class to the auditorium to have a peek. My thirsty eyes were quenched with the spectrum of colors and prizes and what seemed like mile-high displays of what could be possible for me. We walked in silence as all good youngsters did in parochial school back then. Line by line, each of us peering up at the counters that loomed like skyscrapers from our perspective. I thought how odd—silent gayety. And then I saw it in all its majesty. Poised and tall in elegance and it was looking right at me. There was something about this giraffe that made me feel happy, free, lost in contentment and I could not shift my gaze. A sort of knowing occurred—it would be mine. This giant stuffed giraffe would definitely be mine. I thought, I must hurry home and tell my mother that I want to buy it never realizing that it could only be mine in a game of chance. A spinning wheel with numbers—black, white, red. When our teacher explained that in order to take home my dream animal, I'd need to play a game of chance, I was not deterred. I knew it would be mine. Now, some may say this was the foolishness of a child's wishful thinking but, looking back, I truly believe my power of intention was bigger than anyone could have imagined.

I couldn't wait to get home and tell my mother the treasure I had found. It was all I could do to contain myself when I saw her. I chattered and chattered the whole walk home from school. I described every inch of this life-sized creature. Lost in my excitement, as if shaken out of a dream, the expression on my mother's face stilled me. I was confused. I expected excitement and jubilation. Instead, my mother explained that it would be only by chance that I might have this giraffe and that winning was the slightest of possibilities. And, because of its grand size, she warned that I would have no way of getting it home. I was crushed. How could she say these things? Didn't she know that I was to have this? Didn't she know that I would win? Didn't she know that I possessed the ability to make my intentions real?

In retrospect, I understand she didn't intend to hurt my feelings or dash my hopes, but rather to enlighten me to the fact that it was a game of chance and there was a possibility that I would not win. Sometimes life's possibilities can be hard to come to terms with. As adults we have experienced our share of disappointments, but these too are lessons to build upon. (More about this later.)

Well, I would hear none of it. With a sick feeling in my stomach and an ache in my heart, I would not even entertain the thought of my giraffe not coming home with me. I looked at it, it looked at me and that was that…destiny. I lay in bed that night and envisioned how I would win, the sights, the sounds, the smells, came to life. And I saw myself carrying it home as it took its place watching over me next to my bed. In my mind's eye I already owned that giraffe and already felt the joy. The anxiety of getting the giraffe was inconsequential.

The next morning, before going to school, my mother gave me money to play the game so that I could collect my fortune. She wished me luck, to temper her words of warning which were intended to keep me from getting a broken heart. Sitting in class that morning just waiting to go to the carnival seemed more than an eternity to me. Bubbling with excitement, our class headed down. I left my friends and made a beeline for the spinning wheel. And there it was…just waiting for me. Waiting, waiting again. Oh, when would my turn be? "Oh, please God," I prayed, "don't let her win," as the child ahead of me spun the wheel. Finally, my turn. This is it. I put 25 cents on number seven. That was the number given to the giraffe. If the wheel landed on number seven when it stopped, I would take home my prize! Well, I spun, and spun and then spun, again. Feeling slightly worn, my determination only grew taller; tall enough to touch the tip of the giraffe's nose. The carnival worker commented on how much I must have wanted that giraffe. And then as if all the stars and moon listened to my thoughts and conspired together, I won! I felt golden and that perhaps I even possessed the ability to make my thoughtful desires materialize.

Now I know about the law of averages and all that, and sometimes when I think back, I often wonder if the carnival worker didn't take pity on this slight and hopeful child. No matter the circumstances, it all started with the intention, drive and persistence of one little girl that created her own reality. With a little help, I carried my grand prize home that day and was met with my mother's amazement at such a sight. My giraffe was my roommate until it grew old and dusty and even then I kept the tail for I couldn't bear to part with my magical friend. And still today, as a grown woman with two children of my own, my heart feels a lilt whenever I see that four-legged, slender creature and recall the great lesson it had to teach me.

Well right about now you may be saying this is a lovely story, but if the moral is that all we need do is make a wish or want something badly enough in order to get the life we dream of, I must be crazy. Yes, it does take more than that. It all starts with an intention. I intended to win the giraffe and I did. But many times we get ahead of ourselves and mentally run through and project all the possible difficulties that we get defeated before we've even begun. This kills our intention.

Wouldn't it be nice to design our lives and live by intention? To be able to create these wonderful moments again and again just because we wanted to? So consider this…What if setting powerful intentions for the highest good, coupled with taking inspired actions could naturally attract unexpected and unimaginable gifts?

Let's uncover how, by starting with a simple exercise to jog your memory for those moments when you've experienced the flow of intention.

Close your eyes and think about a time when you had a particular desire, intention or goal.

   *Was it a desire to help solve a problem?
   *Be an outstanding leader at work?
   *Live without debt?

In your mind, recreate how you got there. Look and listen for all the details.

*Was it a one-time event or series of events?
*What were the sounds, the sights, the smells, your feelings?
*What was it that made your intention materialize?
*What was the thought process involved?
*What type of action did you take?
*How vividly did you imagine your goal/dream?
*How did you keep it alive every day?
*Did you share your thoughts and desires?

Revel in the moment.

Now that you are in *that place,* let's take a look at a process that can support you in living your intentions.

The 10 Steps of Intention

Step 1: Set the Intention:

An intention is usually broader than a goal, but definitely has some type of outcome. For instance, my intention is to use my gifts of intuition and compassion to heal and inspire people. One of the ways I do this is through writing.

An intention can define the type of person you aspire to be, the way in which you want to lead your life, or it can be a way of defining an event. An example of an event could be a business meeting. I have set the intention for meetings and then shared it with all the participants. For instance, when scheduling a meeting of two departments who more than likely have their own agendas, intentions might look like: focusing on the outcome of the joint project; a meeting environment that is respectful and courteous; highlighting the strengths that each department can deploy to complete the joint project. It's amazing how it focuses the direction and actions of the group. And while I gave an example earlier of myself as a child wanting to acquire something, an intention usually has a tie to a higher purpose. My illustration is intended to highlight the innocence we possessed as children and how this gift and the process of intention lies within each of us today.

Action To Take: What does your heart say? Before even getting to time, money or scheduling issues, sit with your desire, your intention in the light that everything is possible. So, take a moment and think. Do you want to go back to school to get a degree that supports your talents? Do you want to write a book to share knowledge or encouragement? Do you want to be independent and own your own company? Do you want to have more time for you so that you can be your best you?

Step 2: Breathe Life Into Your Intention

Feel it, live it, breathe it, as if it actually has happened. How do you stand? How do you walk when you are living your intention? How do you dress? How do you talk and act? This is so important to get lost in the details of how it feels for it to be real. And it's a great tool to use when we do encounter roadblocks up ahead.

Action To Take: I highly suggest daydreaming. I believe daydreaming is a form of meditation. It's a place where the mind focuses one thing and suspends all else. It creates fertile ground for creativity. Spend time visioning your life and write down your intention in great detail as if it has already occurred. Where can you post it so that you can view it as a daily reminder of where you are going? Some suggestions: computer, calendar, bathroom mirror, car visor, make-up case, refrigerator door. Try creating a vision folder and fill it with words and pictures that represent the fruition of your intention.

Step 3: Give Your Intention Wings

When you begin to verbalize your dreams, it's as if you give them permission to grow wings and fly. Send them out to the universe by sharing your vision and intentions. Research has discovered that goals that are talked about and shared are more likely to be achieved. It is so powerful to hear your own voice speak your intentions out loud.

Action To Take: When you think about sharing your dreams, who is the first person to come to mind? Create your very own support system with like-minded people, loved ones, friends, co-workers or a neighbor. Perhaps this support group could help each other and meeting once a month, sharing and encouraging the process. Or have an email or telephone buddy that you call or calls you at a certain time and day. This could be a 3-5 minute pick me up that boosts your energy.

Step 4: Take Inspired Actions

In order to have your intentions become reality a plan of action needs to go into place. What do you need to have happen? What steps are necessary to take place? What timeline can be given to each step? What type of support will you need? Do you need to hire help? Barter services? Scale back activities? Rev up your exercise plan?

Action To Take: Every day take a step toward your dream. A step can be a micro step (i.e., making a phone call) or a macro step (de-cluttering your environment). Break it down and make it simple. Every little step adds up to big ones, so if you feel overwhelmed, think micro. Even the simple task of making a list, writing down your thoughts and daydreaming are each action steps. Remember, that which becomes reality, begins with thought.

Step 5: The Art of Attraction

When we begin to believe and take steps to become our intentions the universal laws of attraction work with us. You will notice serendipitous events and suddenly attract opportunities that will foster your dreams.

Action To Take: Remember earlier you did all that visioning and creativity? Well, now you get to use that and every day act as though it has already happened. Remember playing pretend? Now you get to do it as a grown up. For instance, if you are interested in writing a fiction novel, research what publications or websites fiction writers frequent. Then subscribe. Is there a group of writers that meet or converse? Join it. Put yourself in situations and environments that will support your intentions. This will open up doors of information and opportunity.

Step 6: Make Room For More

The wheels are turning and you are beginning to see evidence that the universe is supporting your dreams. How can you create more of this? Eliminate and remove the energy drains and things in your life that no longer fit. The habits, clutter and yes, sometimes relationships, that no longer serve you living the life of your intentions.

Action To Take: When you remove physical and mental clutter from your life you are practicing extreme self-care. This self-care can seem uncomfortable at first, but when you start to feel the benefits (more restful, more focus, happier, healthier) you will want to do it more and more. Clean out old papers, old clothes, organize a cabinet. When you make more space in your environment you are inviting new energy and opportunities into your life. When you become more organized you create more time. With that time you've gained you can put more self-care practices into place. One might be, just sitting silently and doing nothing. This too can be uncomfortable at first for seasoned multi-taskers. But, this isn't wasting time at all. It's creating space for new things to enter your life.

Step 7: The Art of Focus

Many times it can be a challenge to stay focused. Distractions occur by our own making (self-talk) and at other times the world seems to challenge us. The purpose of having a written plan, intention statement or visual cue is to bring us back to center. Meditation is an excellent tool you can use to get focused again.

Action To Take: Close your eyes and ask yourself if there is anything you can do to change the outcome or dispel the possible roadblock that is challenging you right now. If so, and it furthers your vision, take action and go for it. If not and it's merely fear-based, cast it aside, thank the contributor (even if it is yourself) and shift your focus back to living your intention. Go back to your vision folder and intention statement to readjust your mindset.

Step 8: Find the Gifts

It's easy to be grateful for things that go our way, but true treasures can be found when we are grateful for the challenges too. Use roadblocks as building blocks. They are your teachers, so find the gifts. Often, we have our own time-line of how things in our lives should unfold. This is not, however, always the timeline of the universe. Take delays for example. It's the gift of time—you can use it wisely or squander it by brooding over what hasn't happened yet. Find the gifts, they are there.

Action To Take: Create a gratitude journal and each day spend time entering all those gifts received that day. Share your gratitude—let others know you are grateful for them because like attracts like. Light a candle at the end of the day and create your very own gratitude ceremony.

Step 9: Think Bamboo

Did you know that bamboo is the material of choice for building in tropical environments? Why is this important to know? Because bamboo is supple. It bends and conforms to whichever way a tropical storm may blow. Sometimes when we want something so dearly we become inflexible. As things change in our lives, so must we. The key is to not get attached, but rather listen to and move in the direction that unfolds. Attachment to the "how" and to the results closes down your intuition and your actions are no longer guided toward a highest good, but rather the wants of the ego. Think bamboo.

Action To Take: So how do you know the difference? Your intuition is your guide. Sometimes it's difficult to discern between your intuition and the conversations in your head. The difference is that intuition is grounded in your gut; the solar plexus. It's not just thoughts and words; it's a knowing feeling. How do you find it? Again, spend time in silence. If you find meditation a challenge, just sit and stare at a focal point and suspend all mind chatter. If your mind starts talking again, gently focus back on what you are staring at. Another exercise is to sit with your eyes closed and listen to the silence. Listen hard. Your intuition will receive the answers and guide you.

Step 10: Celebrate

The gift of life is too special not to celebrate the fact we are here each and every day. Honor yourself for the grace and courage to live with intention.

Action To Take: Acknowledge your growth and where you are today. Maybe your celebration is spending time with loved ones or time alone with nature. Be your own cheerleader. Poise your heart on your own 'giraffe' and focus on what it will take to make it your prize to enjoy forever.

Creating Your Intentions
Written By Crescendo Associates: Patti Bloom and Fred Strauss

Is life getting you down? Do you have a clear vision of what you need in your life to feel successful? Do you feel as if your goals are being accomplished? Have you thought about making changes in your life, but you're not sure how to go about it?

Do any of these questions make you squirm? If your answer is "yes," then you may be ready to make a commitment to make changes in your life. Evaluating your "Intentions" is the next step and the key to your success.

Babies begin their lives with motivation and intention. Their physical and sensory needs must be met in order to survive. Babies are fascinated by adventure and discovery; these concepts are inherent in their daily growth. Children use innovative approaches to solving problems every day. As they grow and experience life through trial and error, children discover which behaviors limit them; and which behaviors and methods will enrich their lives.

For some adults, learned behaviors and methods of advancing through life need tweaking from time to time. Dependency, safety and predictability of life can cause a person to vacillate between the desire to change and the need to remain the same. You may feel a craving for something but might be reluctant to pursue it because you are not clear if satisfying that craving will lead to the quality of life you seek.

Understanding how intentions influence your life can help you define your goals, and guide your adventurous course to your destination.

The topics covered in this chapter include:

- Uncovering your life's purpose
- Identifying your talents and skills
- Defining your intentions
- Developing a plan to realize your intentions
- Steering your course of action
- Identifying obstacles in your path
- Guidance to overcoming obstacles

Why is Intention Important?

Sometimes you meet people who are confident, happy and seem to have a zest for life. They have a positive outlook, seek adventure and are full of enthusiasm. They are genuinely authentic and fully enjoy what they are doing and with whom they are doing it. These people appear to have a deep sense of inner calm and joy that comes from their innermost core.

When you meet such people, you realize that they know who they are, and that what they do is synergistic with their purpose in life. You feel that they know what they want (goals) and have figured out how to achieve it (outcomes). These people, who might be viewed "to have it all," really may have discovered their path through "intention" long ago. This level of awareness enables them to exercise free will and make choices critical for insuring a desired result. Through harnessing your ability to make "intention" a part of your life, you can have joy, feel satisfied with yourself, and improve your personal and professional relationships.

For every person and every unique situation, an innovative approach toward designing a personalized plan for intentions must be developed. There is no one cookbook solution or single method for making this a reality. Accomplishing intentions requires effort and honesty with yourself. Your thoughts, emotions, and spirit need to be balanced and in alignment to work together for your intentions to be actualized.

Definition of Intention

We use many words to describe intentions such as purpose, desires, plans, aims, and objectives. Webster's New Universal Unabridged Dictionary (deluxe second edition) defines intention (L. intendere) as 1. purpose, a stretching or bending of the mind. Intention is manifest when the mind, with great earnestness, and of choice, fixes its view on any idea, considers it on every side, and will not be called off by ordinary solicitation of other ideas (Locke). 2. A determination to do a specified thing or to act in a particular manner.

Based upon the two definitions, every intention begins with an idea which then generates activity to fulfill the objective. For example, the telephone was created with the intention of enabling communication between people with a hearing disability. The objective was communication between two people. The intention set Alexander Graham Bell on a path of activities which resulted in the invention of the telephone. From having intention, Alexander Graham Bell is forever recorded in history as a great inventor.

Therefore, if you have an internal vision of what you want, the fortitude and determination and a "never-give-up-attitude," you are a person with intention. You have the ingredients necessary to accomplish your life goals.

Probing Questions

Your journey starts here. It is always a good idea to begin by evaluating your readiness to commit to any project, no matter the scope. A self evaluation of this type will take some time and effort, but will yield a result greater than the effort you put in.

The following exercises have been designed for you to determine your present level of intention at work, school, financially, emotionally, and spiritually and your readiness to move forward. The first two questions will help you determine where you are now. Be honest with yourself and take the time to fully assess your answers. Write down your responses, so that at the end of your journey you can look back and see how far you have come.

1. Who am I? (Consider describing your unique attributes, qualities, and characteristics which best describe you. This is not a Resume, and does not include what you do.)

2. What is my purpose—Why am I here? (Consider focusing on the reason you are here on Earth, and what you wish to accomplish.)

The next eight questions are designed for you to evaluate your commitment to this undertaking. Your responses are critical toward setting your individual aspirations to improve the quality of your life. Continue to write your answers to the following questions. As you later evaluate the outcome of these exercises, you will find the information invaluable.

1. Do I have the desire to invest time and energy in myself and do I believe in myself?

2. Can I see the difference between where I am now and where I want to be?

3. Am I willing to take full responsibility and make choices and decisions for where I am in my life?

4. Do I recognize my strengths, weaknesses and abilities?

5. Am I fully willing to do the work required to help me reach my goal?

6. Am I willing to be open to try new things, even if I am not absolutely convinced they will work?

7. Am I willing to address the issues and situations that might be holding me back?

8. Do I have the patience and self confidence to take consistent action to move forward to attain my goals?

Creating Your Vision

"We shall not cease from exploration, and the end of all our exploring will be to arrive where we started and know the place for the first time."—T.S. Elliot

It can be difficult to begin a journey into uncharted territory. Some approaches to solving problems include self-help, meditation and psychotherapy. Most traditional therapeutic methods focus on the clients' current behavioral issues. What is necessary to facilitate personal growth is to identify your vision and life's purpose. Your intention will be a natural product of your beliefs and desires.

In my (Patti) personal life, I've experienced the difference between an emotional response to my situation and a plan which was well thought out, based on my intentions. As a child, I had a vision for a unique career. I actually gave it a name (music therapy). Those closest to me thought my idea was unrealistic and placed obstacles in my path to impede my success. My initial reaction to their lack of support was to believe that they were right, and I should give up my pursuit of this dream. I was disappointed that my family did not encourage me in my career aspiration. Shortly afterwards, one of my favorite teachers challenged me to go after my dream. She supported me, and helped me to understand that my life's purpose (intention), to integrate music as a tool to help rehabilitate handicapped people, was worthwhile.

Having gained the insight of my intentions, I was able to focus my intellectual energy into making the vision of becoming a music therapist a reality. At the point where I set my intention into action, I was able to put into perspective the concerns of my family. This enabled me to overcome the obstacles set before me, and allowed me to work on fulfilling my dream. It opened a window into myself which gave me confidence, determination, persistence and the strength to believe in my abilities and intentions. As I look back while writing this story, I understand and value the constant support and guidance that my teacher provided. She was my first coach.

"Everyone has his own specific vocation or mission in life to carry out a concrete assignment which demands fulfillment. Therein he cannot be replaced, nor can his life be repeated. Thus, everyone's task is as unique as is his specific opportunity to implement it."—Victor Frankl, *Man's Search For Meaning*

The following section is designed to assist you in understanding the concept of intention within yourself:

Phase 1—The Mind—This step requires that you begin to train yourself to listen to your mind. In each of us there is a constant battle raging between the mind, emotions and the ego. To fully use the power of intention, tune into your thoughts and focus on the vision that it creates. Try disconnecting from your ego. This takes patience and practice. Be kind and understanding of yourself.

Phase 2—The Emotions—Once you understand what it that your mind is telling you, the next step is to direct it toward your emotions and feelings. This can be tricky; the goal is to acknowledge that your thoughts are in control of your emotions; not the other way around. Our natural tendency is to allow our emotions to react to external events. At this point in your familiar behavior pattern, you might find your emotions are in control of your thoughts. Try this technique: When our children behave in an emotional manner, we often tell them to "use your head" or "think before you speak." As adults, if we want to realize our potential, we can heed our own advice.

Phase 3—Balance—Have you accomplished the first two phases? Congratulations! The next step is to internalize and master the process. This means doing what you love and loving what you do. Balance, combined with discipline, guides your ability to focus and be patient. Your mind is in balance and harmony with your emotions. Neither mind nor emotion has control over you; they have ceased their fight with each other. There is a new source of energy and a unity of purpose.

Phase 4—Intentions—You have identified your requirements for change. To accomplish your intentions, you must believe it is possible, have a plan of action and execute the plan. At this point, your intentions are in control. By making clear your intentions, your world is full of potential. Intentions lead you to feel complete, satisfied and filled with purpose.

As a result, you feel a sense of inner calmness and adventure. You discover you have more energy. You waste less time worrying about what might, or should have been. You are totally aware of what is important and how to attain it. You are the master of what your intentions dictate.

Steps and Activities Fundamental to the Process

1. **Take an Inventory of Yourself**

    The first step in the process of intention is to know where you are and how you got there. Therefore, you must take a personal inventory so you can become cognizant of who you are. By performing a self-assessment, you begin to create the foundation upon which the following activities are predicated. It is critical that during this activity you are totally open and honest with yourself, and trust that the outcome will lead you to connecting with your inner self.

    It is not necessary for you to complete this self assessment in a single sitting. However, allocating sufficient time and committing to complete this within a defined timeframe will insure that it is completed. Before beginning these tasks have paper and a pen handy.

    The following steps will help you organize and collect the information for your inventory:

    a. Determine how much time you spend during a single sitting to concentrate without losing focus. You may want to start with a short time period (not more than 15 minutes), and incrementally increase it over time.
    b. On the top of a blank page, write what area of your life you want to focus on. Some suggested areas are: family and friends, creativity and talents, work, leisure activities, spiritual (beliefs), emotional (self-worth, self-confidence, self-esteem), intellectual pursuits, physical and health, and financial.
    c. Find a quiet place where you will not be disturbed during the time you spend focusing on this task. The purpose here is to utilize your ability, desire and willingness to connect with and describe your inner world.
    d. Contemplate on the area which you have selected to assess. Place all your thoughts on that area and be an observer of your own thoughts. You cannot discover your awareness if you are contemplating things that are not relevant. If stray thoughts come into your mind, do not focus on them. Simply pay no attention and let them disappear.
    e. Write your first impressions. Do not criticize, judge, edit, or evaluate them. Simply record your thoughts. Some may seem silly, impossible, painful or even hurtful. All are important, as they play a part of who you are and will provide insight into your intentions.

f. Repeat steps d and e for the areas of your life which you have identi-fied. When you have finished the Inventory, this information will be useful when creating your intentions.

2. Connecting to Your Intentions

Think back on how you answered the questions of "Who am I?" and "What is my purpose?" What feelings did these questions bring up in you? Feelings are a function of what you are thinking, what you are con-templating, and listening to your inner voice (intuition.) Your thoughts and feelings provide clues to your intentions and the potential that is striving to be manifested through your actions.

Once you understand your intentions, you'll be able to establish your goals and action plans to give them expression. By identifying your intentions, you transform your aspirations into reality.

The following steps will help you identify and connect with your intentions.

a. Determine how much time you can spend during a single sitting con-centrating without losing focus (this will vary depending on the indi-vidual.) Be comfortable so that you can address these questions clearly.
b. On the top of each blank page write, "What's missing in my life," the "Circumstances in my life that I would like to change," "What is meaningful in my life now," "What others want from me," and "What I want for my life in the future?"
c. Find a quiet place where you will not be disturbed for that period of time. Your desire is to your willingness and ability to connect with and describe your inner world. Sit in a comfortable position.
d. Complete writing your list. Concentrate on one question at a time. If something comes into your mind that relates to another question, make a note of it and move on. When creating your personalized list of your life's passions, remember that the scope of this task is multi-dimensional. Any purpose you identify has a concurrent impact on a multitude of areas in your life. In order for your passions to become an intention, they must be relevant in all domains of your life.
e. Use your responses to the questions you just created and your responses from Step 1 and now organize your thoughts and capture your unique set of intentions on paper. Next, ask yourself the following questions: "Given my life now, and if these intentions were fulfilled,

would my life's purpose be complete?" If your answer is "no" then repeat the steps necessary for you to answer in the affirmative.

f. Make your intention simple and to the point. Your intention does not have to be complicated to be valid. If it contains more than one thought, decompose it into multiple pieces.

g. Express it in your own words. Be sure that your intentions resonate and represent who you truly are. No one can explain your intentions better than you can. Your writings should be composed in your own unique style. Try not to let your intellect and emotions conflict with what you are saying. The more you believe in your intentions, the easier it will be to create a set of goals to realize your potential.

3. Set Your Goals

Once you have compiled your list of intentions, it is necessary to take steps toward making them a reality. Using your list of intentions, you and your coach can co-create a set of clear goals. A goal is an intention with a definite objective. The goals you establish must be specific, measurable, action oriented, positive, realistic, challenging, and attainable.

Your goals will act as a guide to move you along the path towards your objectives. Your goals can also serve to correct your course if you stray off your path.

4. Perform Pre-Assessment

To measure the magnitude and impact of change in your life derived from fulfilling your intention, you need to perform a pre-assessment. Identify the desired set of outcomes for each intention which you have delineated. Include with each goal the intended outcome and the method for measuring the impact on your life's purpose.

5. Create Action Plan

Now that you have a clear set of goals and measurements for your intentions, you need to plan a way to achieve them. First, list the possible ways which can be used to achieve your goals. Next, identify and list the activities necessary to support the attainment of each goal. Then, for each activity, list the set of tasks that must be accomplished to satisfy that particular goal. Each task should have an associated timeframe required to accomplish it.

Your action plan should include your main plan, as well as a contingency plan. This is advisable in the remote chance that your primary plan can not be accomplished. By working with your coach, you can select the most feasible way to work towards achieving your goals.

6. Execute Action Plan

Now that you know what you want and how to get it, it's time to take action. Each activity and task that has been identified must be executed. During this step, keep your focus on the goals that you need to complete in order to fulfill your intentions. The two sections which follow the Process of Intention discuss obstacles, how they may prevent you from achieving your goals, and how to overcome them.

7. Perform Post-Assessment

Once you have implemented your plan of action, the next step is to perform a post-assessment. Using your intentions, list of goals, and pre-assessment outcomes; identify the goals that have been accomplished, the ones which are still in progress, and those which have not yet been met.

8. Evaluate Results

The purpose of this step is to analyze the post-assessments in order to determine what was accomplished. The objective is to identify those actions which were successfully completed and made a positive contribution to your life; and those actions which were incomplete, unsuccessful or had a negative impact on your life.

Create a table with three columns: "Successful—Continue Doing;" "Unsuccessful—Should Be Changed;" and "Changes That Need to Be Made." Based upon your post-assessment results, fill in this table. You may also want to indicate the importance of each entry.

9. Implement Changes/Improvements

The last step is to implement the changes you identified and continue the process. Remember, most people do not get it right the first time. Recall the number of failures that Abraham Lincoln had in his life before he became President. Abraham Lincoln eventually fulfilled his intention to be a great leader, and moved the United States and the world forward. In the face of adversity, Mr. Lincoln persevered.

Obstacles in Your Path Toward Intentions

"Courage is not the absence of fear; rather, it is the ability to take action in the face of fear."—Nancy Anderson, *Work With Passion*

Obstacles can have negative, as well as positive outcomes, depending on how you choose to direct their paths. On the negative side, an obstacle is debilitating or sometimes paralyzing. We derail our intentions by substituting excuses for not pursuing them. On the positive side, obstacles generate within us the motivation and drive necessary to move forward on our path toward intention.

The following list is a sample of some common obstacles, or excuses you may find yourself using to impede your progress:

1. **Fear**

    Fear is paralyzing only if you let it be. Fear is an obstacle only if you let it control your life. Don't let fear be the focus of what prevents you from turning your intention into a reality. Fear prevents us from harnessing the energy we need to realize our potential.

2. **Avoidance**

    Avoidance will hurt your success rate. When you find yourself at an impasse, stop and ask yourself "What am I avoiding and how will it prevent me from reaching my goal?"

3. **Seeking Approval and Consent**

    Seeking approval and consent from people whose opinion you value. Having support from people whose opinion you value is wonderful, but their opinion should not be the criterion for achieving your dream. Trust in yourself and give yourself permission to succeed. Norman Vincent Peale said, "Change your thoughts and you change your world."

4. **Perfection and Indecision**

    Perfection and indecision is dangerous if you are waiting for the perfect time, place and circumstances to begin working on your intentions. Decide to take the risk. As you move along, you will learn and improve with every step. If you wait too long, your enthusiasm may be lost.

5. **No Time for the Dream**

    No time for the dream sets up a self-fulfilling prophecy. Being reluctant to invest your time and resources in your dream (intentions) can only insure that you won't succeed. This is procrastination. When you procrastinate, you ensure that your dream will be derailed. Make time in your life to work on what you love.

Overcoming Your Obstacles

1. **Take Positive Risk/Take Control of Your Life**

    Nothing is ever achieved by just watching from the sidelines. Life is not a spectator sport. You must be willing to take positive steps towards achieving your goals. Risk goes along with the territory. Believing in yourself and taking action in the face of adversity, will only help you toward your goal. Begin to build your self-confidence and self-worth by taking baby steps; at other times you will have to take giant leaps. Conquer your obstacles and do whatever is within your power to move beyond them.

2. **Stay Motivated**

    The process of turning your idea into reality may take time. The path may not be linear, and you might be tempted to give up. Be persistent. Believe in yourself. By listening to other people's success stories, you can gain encouragement from their experiences. Surround yourself with positive people who believe in you and support your vision. People who nurture your potential for success, and champion your achievements, can be a wonderful source of motivation.

3. **Self-Confidence/Self-Worth/Self-Esteem**

Acting on your intentions will ultimately give you a feeling of achievement. When you take action, you build your self-confidence, self-worth and self-esteem. You gain personal insight into mastering your objectives. It is important to remember that you are your own number one fan. Using your talents as you believe you should, attracts others and inspires them to fulfill their potential as well.

4. **Increasing Your Productivity**

An advantage of overcoming obstacles is learning to manage your time more efficiently and effectively. If you find yourself procrastinating, identify the cause and take action to resolve the issue. Don't give up along the way. You owe it to yourself to try. Napoleon Hill said "it takes a person half their lives to discover that life is a do it yourself project." How you choose to manage your time is essential for the energy you need to increase your productivity. Ultimately, you will have more free time to do the other things in your life which you enjoy.

5. **Your Time Is Now**

You need to keep the promise you made to yourself. Map out a plan and take action. Involve yourself with activities and organizations that can support your beliefs and desires. Begin networking in groups with similar interests to further enhance and expand your vision. Hillel said, "If I am not for me, who will be? If not now, when?"

By defining your intentions, a new and different journey may now take focus in your life. To be successful and fulfill your life's purpose takes time, energy and dedication. This chapter has discussed the benefits of establishing your intentions and describing specific methods needed to uncover your true potential in order to make your dreams a reality.

Discovering and exploring the significance of your life's journey will ultimately lead you to experience yourself at the most intimate level. Your intentions will evolve as you move through life. The journey will be challenging; the rewards will be considerable.

Chapter Two:
Finding The Real You

Finding Your Life Purpose
Written By Lynn B. Engeholm

"To find in ourselves what makes life worth living is risky business, for it means that once we know we must seek it. It also means that without it life will be valueless."
—Marsha Sinetar, *Ordinary People as Monks and Mystics*

It is my firm belief that our primary task is to discover and define our purpose and then to live our life on purpose to the best of our abilities. When we search for our purpose we ask ourselves these questions: "What should I be doing? How can I best be myself? What am I going to give back to the world?" Our discovery of our life purpose evolves over time. Some of us are ready at an early age to journey on this road of discovery. Discovery leads to consciously knowing what is in our heart and soul as to why we were created. However many of us start the journey to discover our purpose and get detoured by living our day to day lives or perhaps living a life according to someone else's agenda. We do not hear the voice of our heart telling us why we were created. We live our lives thinking, doing, and reacting with little time spent on following our heart. Our heart holds the truth about what we value most and what is our life purpose. Our lives most likely are aligned in some way to our life purpose. There are times when our hearts sing loud enough for us to hear and feel the direction we must take. I believe that many of us today are seeking a meaningful life and that contentment is our new bottom line. Being able to articulate your personal life purpose and live with that purpose creates a life that revolves around what you want rather than revolving around the crisis du jour. You will have more time, space, energy, and be focused on what creates joy in your life.

My life purpose is to share my wisdom and inspire others. For me it took a great deal of "soul searching" to be able to identify and express my statement of purpose. Once I had my purpose statement and expressed it to others, I said to myself "Why of course this is me!" I have been doing this all my life but I never expressed it in a statement to myself or others before. It was in my heart. The power of having a personal statement of purpose allows for unlimited possibilities and passion. Articulating my life purpose now adds depth to the journey I am taking. I enjoy working with women and supporting them to be whatever they want to be. With my life purpose visible, I am now thinking of how I can support women by sharing my wisdom. I am asking myself questions like "How can I inspire women to want and achieve more?" I am definitely passionate about the possibilities. I would like to share with you some steps you can take to discover your life purpose. Remember, you want to get in touch with your heart's voice, not what you think you should be doing or what you think your family or friends want you to do. This is about you—why you were created and the gifts you were given to share with others.

How Does One Get In Touch With Life Purpose?

Step 1: Re-establish your integrity. "Integrity is a state of personal wholeness, wellbeing, and fulfillment—not something to achieve, but rather a statement of our being. It is a reflection of who you are in any moment and is the dynamic relationship between purpose and following it on a path. It is the vigilant development, or adjustment, of the fit between our calling and conduct that allows us to sustain a high level of integrity." (Definition used by Coach U., Inc., Introduction to Personal Foundation, www.coachu.com). Integrity is personal and my level of integrity is different from your level of integrity. Integrity means:

- Being your best,
- Being whole as a person,
- Being responsible for what you do and do not do,
- Responding completely to life's lessons, and
- Honoring yourself as an individual and honoring your body.

Following our sense of integrity is a choice we make. This is very similar to living our life on purpose. When we are living our life in integrity and on purpose we change from functioning on automatic pilot or reactive decision making to creating plans or strategies based on what serves us best, brings passion into our life, and shares our talents with others.

Ask yourself these questions to get in-touch with your integrity.

- What is integrity to you?

- Are you in "integrity" right now? If not, why not?

- What do you need to feel whole as a person?

- What does being your best mean to you?

- What is incomplete in your life? What do you need to do to complete what is incomplete?

- How are the aspects of your life (Personal, Professional, Health, Relationships, Financial, and Fun) set-up to work effortlessly? How are they set up to be a great struggle?

Step 2: Connect to your values. "Values are ideals that are personally important and meaningful and draw you forward. Values are inherent; we all have them. They are specific and individual, but people can share common values. For example, people often value honesty, openness, and respect, in a conversation." (Definition used by Coach U., Inc. www.coachu.com) At the end of this chapter is a list of possible additional values that may help you choose the values that mean the most to you. A value is a must for you to be yourself. Ask yourself as you look through the list of values and think of other values "What do I love to do with my time? Say each value and see if it resonates with who you are. Try the value on and see if it fits you comfortably.

When you have your list of values, pick the three or four that mean the most to you now. Write your values here.

Step 3: Look at your talents and strengths. What do you do exceptionally well? What are your natural gifts? Since our strengths and gifts come naturally to us we may take them for granted or may not realize that they are indeed an asset. Ask your friends and family "What are my greatest strengths?" You might be surprised at the responses that you get. Write them down and see which ones feel right to you. Write down the strengths and talents that you feel are truly you.

Step 4: The last step is to ask yourself "What am I most passionate about?" Can you think of three times in your life when you were doing something that you were truly passionate about and you feel you were living on purpose? Write down your memories and see if you note a common theme. What was happening that reflected your passion about the situation?

Look at how your passions align with your integrity, strengths, and values. Is there a common theme that you are beginning to see? Write this down.

Building Your Purpose Statement.

Your purpose is anything that touches your heart and soul and makes a difference to you. It is based on your integrity, values, strengths, and passion. It is important to keep your purpose statement broad to allow for possibilities and passion. Per Marcia Wieder, author or *Making Your Dreams Come True,* here are some examples of purpose statements that answer the question "How do you want to live your life?"

- To adventurously and joyously be creative.
- To embrace life with wonder.
- To live authentically.
- To be loving, compassionate, and free.
- To be a lifelong learner and share my knowledge and experience.

Once you have your statement of life purpose take a moment to feel the passion building inside of you as you say your life purpose to yourself, your family, and to all around you. Start exploring how you are going to start living on purpose each and every day. Let your purpose be your barometer: what enters your life, what remains in your life, and what will no longer be part of your life because it does not fit with your purpose. Set an intention now that you are going to live your life on purpose each day.

For me, living on purpose freed up a great deal of time because I eliminated tasks and obligations that were not aligned with my purpose. What came into my life were choices. My choice was to fill the time with marvelous things that were related to my life purpose. I believe that living life by choice is a very powerful and productive way to live.

There will be times when you will need to refocus on your purpose. Living on purpose requires that you:

- Not let fear stop you,
- Take risks,
- Take action toward your dreams daily, and
- Realize that you are part of a much larger plan.

There will be days of joy and days of anguish. Not being true to your life purpose is not always easy, yet it is rewarding. When you live on purpose, you impact your life and the lives of those around you. This impact ripples out beyond what you define as your individual community. You contribute to a much larger plan through your unique gifts, talents, strengths, values, and purpose.

In summary, getting in touch with your life purpose requires that you look inward to:

- Re-establish your integrity,
- Uncover what you value most in life,
- List your unique talents, gifts, and strengths,
- Discover what you are passionate about, and
- Set an intention that you are going to live on purpose each and every day.

Take time, listen to your heart, and create a statement of life purpose that rings true for you. Write it here.

I encourage you to live with your purpose statement for a period of time, 3-6 months. After that time examine how your life has unfolded. Do you need to change you purpose statement completely? Do you need to change your purpose statement to infuse more passion? The revision may be as easy as adding an adverb as "joyously" or "easily." Per Marcia Wieder, author or *Making Your Dreams Come True*, "When you're standing in your life's purpose, the passion is always there, and possibilities are everywhere. You feel powerful, and capable of making your dreams come true."

Additional List Of Possible Values:

TO BE ADVENTUROUS

Take risks	Try the unknown
Explore	Travel
To speculate	Attempt to do the unfamiliar

TO GUIDE

Be a leader	To inspire others
Be persuasive	To rule
Influence others	Support others

THE LOVE OF BEAUTY

Graceful	Magnificence
Pleasant appearance	Joie de vivre
Artistic	Naturalist

TO BE AN EXPERT

Specialist	Authority
Professional	Connoisseur
Set principles	Superiority

BE A CATALYST

Influence change	Coach
Have an effect	Inspire others
Support others	Encourage others

ENJOY PLEASURABLE THINGS

Fun loving	Blissful
Entertaining	Ecstasy
Sports/Games	Happiness

CONTRIBUTOR

Provider	Make possible
Assist	Make stronger
Concede	Encourage

TO ASSOCIATE

Connected	United
Relate	To cultivate
Part of a family	Part of a community

CREATOR

Designer	Inventor
Imaginative	Original
Visualize	Builder
Inspiration	Bring together

SENSITIVITY

Tender	Affect
Supportive	Responsive
Compassionate	Warmth
Kindliness	Sympathetic

DISCOVERY

To Learn	Observe
To Locate	Realize
Expose	Differentiate

SPIRITUALITY

Conscious	Be tolerant
Connect with God	Sacred
Respect	Passionate

TO EXPERIENCE

Sense	Feel good
Radiance	Understand
Encounter	Sensations

TO EDUCATE

Teach	Explain
Enlighten	Make ready
Prepare	Strengthen

TO SUCCEED

To accomplish	Achieve
Win	Win over
Do well	Attract

Live Your Passion And Experience Your Joy
Written By Kay Dinehart

I truly believe that everyone has come to this planet to play out their purpose. You may ask, what is purpose? I believe it is the things we do that make our heart sing with joy. Our purpose will always include what we value and therefore it is really important to identify our values. Values represent what is most important to us in life. These are a few values you may want to consider: love, courage, freedom, cooperation, gratitude, leadership, learning and having fun.

When we identify what it is we value, we are able to clearly discern our gifts.

Identify 10 things that you value most.

1.

2.

3.

4.

5.

6.

7.

8.

9.

10.

Now, circle 4 that you feel are the most important. Are you living by these values at the present time?

If you are, how does that make you feel?

If not, what steps can you take to do so?

Once you have begun the process of orienting your life around values, you begin to infuse energy into your life.

When we are doing what we love, our energy will soar and we will be full to make our contribution to the planet. Each one of us has strengths and gifts that are unique and valuable. When we work through our strengths using these gifts, we know we are doing what it is we were meant to do. As we explore purpose and passion, I would like you to remember that deep down you know what it is that gets you excited and energized. Sometimes life gets in the way and you forget what your real purpose is. I intend to give you the resources to identify your dreams and passions and help you.

What is it you have always dreamed of doing or being?

From the time we were young children we are told that dreaming is a waste of time. Yet I believe it is the dream that creates our reality. The dreams or visions are what get us excited and when focused, they become the reality that manifests in our lives.

Questions are all important in moving us forward toward our vision. Ask yourself:

"What is it that I really love doing and how can I bring this to the world in a grand vision?"

A grand vision brings our talents forward in a way that enhances the community we live and work in and improves the world in some way. They include a grander vision of final outcome. For instance a company may have a vision of how their product will enhance their consumers as well as the employees working there but when a percentage of profits is donated to charity, the repercussions are world changing. I love the concept of a grand vision because of the trickle down effect. When you are doing what you love other people will catch this energy and they also will be moved toward doing what they love. Haven't we all heard an inspirational speaker who is able to move the whole audience because of his own experience and passion? When people work from a sense of purpose, passion is always evident because the person is energized from the inside out.

What does your life look like?

What do you want it to look like?

What are you tolerating and what can you get rid of?

I find this a good place to begin so that you can get a handle on what is draining your time and energy. Tolerations can be found in all aspects of our life. For your consideration I will list a few that are quite common: a boring job, closets that need cleaning, junk diet, late credit card payments etc. Let's look at what you can eliminate from your life so that you have more time and energy to do what it is you really want. The more things you can eliminate the more time is now available for doing the things you love. I like to look at this as doing a Feng Shui of your life. When you remove the clutter from your life you make the space for other activities that you love doing. Think about your relationships, home, workplace, money issues or anything else that comes to mind that really is draining you.

What are five things you do not enjoy doing?

1.

2.

3.

4.

5.

Now, do some of these things still need to be done? Take the time to think about who you can enlist or hire to help get this accomplished. Can the children help you out with the chores and can you hire someone to do the heavy gardening work? Think about changing the way you have been doing things and make the effort now to do them differently.

Three changes I can make now are:

1.

2.

3.

What is the new outcome I envision as a result of these changes?

What have you come here to do?

What fuels you with passion and excitement?

If you could do whatever you wanted, what would it be?

What are your deepest longings?

Are you here to lead, have adventure, guide, teach, nourish, be of service, create beauty, coach? What is it you have come here to do? I challenge you to identify this purpose now. Think of those times in you life when you were filled with passion and excitement.

Reflect back in time and remember when you were in total joy doing something. Where were you and what were you doing?

What is the thread of commonality between these things? The 'where' is important because it can be the thing that ties these things together. For example, do all your joyous experiences happen outdoors? That may be the common thread that pulls all your passionate experiences together. Could it be that your purpose in life is to be outdoors as often as possible and you have somehow wound up behind a desk doing a job that is not fulfilling? Maybe you bought into someone else's vision of what your life should look like and lost track of your own.

How did this happen and how can you rectify this? First, you must look at some key beliefs you have built your life around. Are these beliefs your choice or were you born into them? Are they working for you at this time and if not are you ready to re-evaluate them. How many of us are doing what our parents did because we thought that was just great? Did you mindlessly assume that their great job would be yours too? Did you really identify your dreams or did you just slide into living someone else's? These are some hard questions that must be addressed as you move toward finding your purpose in life.

Think of 3 beliefs that you were born into that no longer serve you.

1.

2.

3.

Are you ready to let them go?

All great journeys start with a vision. It is the same as when you are planning a vacation. Many questions come up in the initial planning. For example, what kind of a trip do I want and do I want to rest or have a lot of activity? Who will be going with me and do we enjoy doing the same things? This is similar to how we go about planning our life vision. We ask many questions that begin to challenge and excite us at the same time.

We begin to discover what we want and then take steps toward finalizing our plans so that we can get there.

As you begin the process of dreaming a life that infuses passion within, your vision begins to take form. If you have identified your life purpose, how can you bring this forward and share it with others? This is the time to start thinking about how your values can enrich community, family, friends etc. How can these gifts support you financially and what do you need to do to move yourself toward this? What first step is needed now to begin the process of manifesting this vision in the world?

It is all-important at this time to see yourself doing what you love. In your greatest dream what does your life look like and how do you look and feel in this new lifestyle? Think about a time you have created something you were very proud of. First you had the thought and then you took the steps necessary to realize this creation. You may have made a few or many revisions but at last the project reached completion and you were thrilled with the result. Many times when we plan a house project we have followed these steps. How many times when you have decorated a room in your home did you visualize the look and feeling of it? You may have even invited others in for their input and opened yourself to many possibilities to get the best result possible. So it is with our grand life vision, the more possibilities we explore the greater potential for our dream outcome. Walt Disney said," All our dreams come true if we have the courage to pursue them."

The next step you need to take is to describe this vision as clearly as possible. Your thoughts and words now need clarity. As your vision begins to take form, you may be ready to take some baby steps forward…This is the time you must see your vision clearly and speak it whenever possible. You must be able to see and feel this life that you want so very much and take the steps forward no matter what. Your thoughts create reality. At this time be aware of what thoughts are limiting you and change them to empowering ones. Whenever the going gets rough you have your vision and affirmations to keep you going. Positive self talk during this time is all-important. Some things you may want to say to yourself are: "I will succeed, I will take steps forward, and I will stay in my vision until I get there." You are now starting to walk your talk. Be aware of your conversations with people. Are they encouraging? Supportive? If not, consider reducing association with them. Give yourself the gift of creating a positive environment as you walk through this change into your heart-felt vision.

Now, look at where you are and set specific measurable goals to reach the final destination.

What steps will you take to get you through the rough spots? What resources are available to you and who can you find to advise and help you when the going gets tough. This is a great time to take inventory of friends, family and business associates that can support you.

This is a great time to outline your vision and put in place some strategies for getting there.

Vision Outline:

Create your vision. Incorporate as many details as you can. Include Who, What, Where, When, and How.

Strategies for achieving this:

1.

2.

3.

A calendar is a beneficial tool that helps with scheduling and time limitations. It is a great place to check on your progress. It is also important to list things you can do to move this project forward.

What places can I go to and what materials can I read to shorten the time period toward completion of my goals?

1.

2.

3.

Are there new things I can try and where can I find them? What are they?

1.

2.

3.

The more creative you get the more possibilities open to you. The process is just as important as the outcome and the experiences learned are all important. Our experiences are our best teacher. This is a time of trusting as the process unfolds toward the final outcome.

Once the vision is under way, this is a good time to look at your life and evaluate it in terms of balance. Is life balance a part of your grand vision? There are many components that go into creating a full, enriching life. In this exploration, we will take a look at the whole person in terms of body, mind and spirit.

The body is our instrument for navigating in the world. It requires exercise, good food and rest to work effectively and efficiently. How much exercise are you getting? Is this an area that can be worked on or better yet, are you willing to commit to a regimen that can fit comfortably into your lifestyle? During this time of goal setting and scheduling don't forget to keep the body fit and energized. Make a plan and stick to it.

There are many ways we can relieve stress and rest the body during the time that our vision is developing. A good night's sleep is so important in running a full and busy day. This time is exciting and a built in routine is always the most beneficial for optimum efficiency. Meditation is another excellent tool many use to minimize stress. It helps in quieting the mind so that we can energize and re-fuel and refocus. I believe that even brief time-outs during the day can be beneficial to productivity. Another great stress reliever is the practice of deep breathing. When we take a few deep breaths, we are oxygenating our bodies which, again, enhances our energy. I can't stress how important self-care is during this very busy time of change and growth.

The mind needs to be harnessed to create the life we intend. When focusing the mind on a vision, we are able to move our thoughts in a positive, constructive way. Clear focus and vision are all important in the creation process. It is up to you to change the thoughts that don't serve you and close down possibilities for success. The questions to focus on are:

What do I want?

How will I get there?

Finally our spirit is that quiet voice within that knows. It can always be identified through feelings. If it doesn't feel good, we must honor that feeling. When we feel dread in the pit of our stomach it is a clear signal of danger and when our heart sings we are in joy and doing what we love. I believe we have all come to this world to be in joy doing our life purpose. Sometimes we get lost in others belief systems or expectations and they begin to feel very uncomfortable. By listening to our own inner voice and recognizing our own wisdom we can begin to do the work we were meant to do on this remarkable life journey. Life is truly a gift to be treasured.

Baby Steps To A Big Vision
Written By Maris Tain

"The future belongs to those who believe in the beauty of their dreams."
—Eleanor Roosevelt

Welcome to the land of dreams. Have you ever had a vision so crystal clear that you were actually able to see into your future? This is not a fairytale, nor a crystal ball story. This is about you, and the real possibilities that you have the power to create when you have a clear, strong vision of your future. With this vision, you can be on the road to your dreams in just a matter of time.

What will you need to create your vision?

- Time
- A Journal (with beauty that will inspire your innermost thoughts) and Pen,
- Or Computer
- Optional: voice or audio tape recorder, flip chart and marking pen, a partner, a coach, or someone you trust to share the journey you are about to embark on.

Vision, Clarity, Passion, and Dreams:

You don't have to believe in fairytales to believe that your dreams can come true. All you have to do is have a vision. Vision, combined with clarity and passion opens all possibilities of your dreams becoming your reality. Add a significant amount of belief and commitment, with a dash of abundance and love, and your dreams will be within reach sooner than you think.

Vision is an imagined destination created by your hopes and dreams that propels you to move toward it. Vision combined with passion and commitment inspires you to leap forward on your journey with excitement and enthusiasm to turn that vision into reality. When you are connected to your vision, it guides your actions much like a candle lights your way in the dark, and leads you straight down the road to living your dreams. *Do you have a vision for your life? Are you truly connected to that vision?*

Clarity as defined by the dictionary is "Clearness of thought or style; lucidity, free from obscurity and easy to understand; the comprehensibility of clear expression, the quality or state of being clear." *Are you clear in which direction your life is moving? Or are you faced with many roads not knowing which way to turn?*

Passion, if you have ever experienced it, is a powerful intense emotion, like true happiness, love, or joy with such boundless enthusiasm, that it made your heart quicken with the memory of it. *Can you imagine waking each day feeling the excitement of knowing that what you will be doing that day will be fueled with all that gives you that kind of joy?*

Dreams (for our purposes) is a condition or achievement that is longed for; a deep aspiration...one that is exceptionally gratifying, exquisite, or beautiful. *Are you living the life you have always dreamed of? Or are you living the life that someone else has dreamed for you?*

Think about a time that you have had a dream, a deep aspiration in your life that was so big and so clear that you knew exactly where you wanted to go and how to get there. Have you ever had a dream so filled with passion that it excited and inspired you enough to do whatever it took to propel you toward it? If you have, then you can understand how having a vision for your life can lead you down the road to your dreams. Discover one dream, and you may uncover an endless array of possibilities.

Having a crystal clear vision can move you closer to your purpose and living your dreams.

"Nothing happens unless first a dream is created."—Carl Sandberg

Your vision is what guides you to move in the right direction towards accomplishment and fulfillment, joy, and living your dreams. Are you living your life with the true joy you deserve? Or, are you following the map that was created by others such as your parents or other family, or even negative life experiences that left you with limiting self beliefs, the beliefs that lead you to stand in your own way? Have you ever heard yourself say, "I can't make money doing what I love." "I'm not creative enough." Or, "Making such a major change at this point in my life is too hard or scary." Or, perhaps you have been led by other outside influences like newspapers, community, culture, or society that says you should act and be a certain way, a way that may not be satisfying or fulfilling?

These are self limiting beliefs and it is necessary that you believe that you, and only you have the power to change it.

How do you get to this place of living your life vision, the life of your dreams?

The first thing you need to do is begin taking time just for you. Oh, I can just hear your negative mind talk. "How can I take time just for me? I have my very busy and demanding career; I have a family; I have a calendar that looks like a roadmap." But, where is that roadmap leading you? How can you not take time just for you? What is the cost if you don't take time for you? If you are stressed, if you are not feeling fulfilled, if you are not filled with joy every day, think of how that affects not only you and your personal well-being, but your family and friends, and the people you come in contact with everyday.

Think what difference you can make in your own life if you were living your dreams. And just imagine the influence you will have on your children or those close to you as you recreate yourself as their role model to follow their hearts.

Your Time:

Take time for yourself. Take time for some deep reflection. Imagine your life is just how you want it. You are living from day to day with an attitude of abundance, love and joy. You are filled with calmness and tranquility. Your relationships are satisfying and filling you up. You are loving every minute of your working day. Your career is your passion. Everything you do in your life is reflecting your values. You are living your true priorities. In a Perfect World only, you say? Well, maybe, but when you can truly say you are following that all-important roadmap to your dreams, you can then say you are living successfully. You understand the meaning of your life and why you are here on earth. You will then, and only then, be creating the life of your vision, and then, living the life of your dreams.

So now that you have decided to take some time for yourself, give yourself a pat on the back. And let's take a few moments for a short journey, a visualization through which you will be able to create your vision of the future. You may want to record this in a soft, reflective tone so you can play it back to yourself. Then you can hear you encouraging you to really feel your "perfect life". As you ask yourself each question, and as you say each thought-provoking statement, pause for a few moments and reflect on the first few things that come into your awareness. I suggest you have a new and inspiring journal nearby so you can jot down some of the things you experience that will light up your being.

Arrange some quiet time when you can be alone and not be disturbed. Take the phone off the hook (and please don't forget to turn off your cell phone too.) Now, find your favorite chair or sofa and get comfortable, (but, please don't get too comfortable. This is not naptime.)

Visualization—Living The Life You Love:

(To get the most from this short meditation, please have someone read it to you, or read it to yourself slowly, pausing after each thought, and allowing yourself to go wherever it takes you.)

So as we begin, close your eyes, take a few deep breaths, and let them out slowly. Breathe in deeply, and slowly exhale. Breathe in again, and again, slowly let it out. Breathe in deep one more time, and as you slowly exhale, begin to notice the stress of the day leave your body. Feel your body relaxing. Focus on your breath and feel each muscle from head to toe beginning to relax. With your eyes closed, become aware of all that is around you. The air in the room—is it moving or still? Is it warm or cool? Become aware of the clothes you are wearing and the chair or couch you are sitting on.

You will have thoughts coming in and out of your awareness. Let them come and then let them go. No need to fight them, just notice them, notice that there is a beginning and an end to each thought. And, there is space in between the thoughts. Notice this space between the thoughts and allow it to get wider and wider until this space between the thoughts is bigger than each thought and eventually is all that is in your awareness. It may seem like this space is a space of nothingness, but it is really the space of your essential awareness. It is the essence of who you really are. There is no ego in this space. There is no stress in this space. There is no negative mind-talk in this space. There is no emotion in this space. It is just the space where you are completely aware, feeling whole and at peace. *(It may take several attempts for you to fully experience this, but the more you practice, the easier it becomes to access this space of peace and complete awareness.)*

As you feel the calmness and tranquility in this space of awareness, slowly go back in time and think of lost passion. Has there ever been something you have longed to have or longed to do in your life? Something you may have promised yourself you'd do when "you grow up," but now never seem to have the time for. Have you ever had a passion that you wished you could turn into a career, but someone along your path squashed your dream? Be aware of the feelings this passion generates in your consciousness. Remember the excitement this passion brought to every corner of your being.

Now imagine you are living your absolute perfect life. Is this passion a part of that perfect life? Imagine awaking each day excitedly looking forward to what the day holds. And as you awake, you know each day holds an adventure that ignites your being and lights up your soul. Feel the immeasurable joy that fills you up. (Remember to read slowly and pause between each question or statement giving you time for reflection.)

What is happening in this perfect life? What are you doing? How are you feeling? What are you passionate about? Imagine you are loving every minute of your work day whether it is going well or not as expected. Imagine in detail what you are doing in your job that keeps you so very excited. Imagine you are so passionate about your career that you would be willing to do it for free.

Who is in your life? Imagine that each and every person you welcome into your life is someone who raises your level of positive energy, raises your level of consciousness, and adds to your joy. What and Who are your sources of positive energy? What are you giving? And what are the gifts you are receiving in return? Are you having fun? What is creating your pure joy? Relish in this joy you are feeling. And know that it is you that has arranged this perfect life.

Acknowledge that there may be disappointments in this perfect life, but that each is handled with an "Attitude of Gratitude," focusing on all you are grateful for, all that is good in your life. Each disappointment and any negative life experiences are welcomed and become a lesson for growth. Imagine you are living from a very positive place of abundance and love, knowing that your glass is always at least half full and you truly know that life is good. You are living your perfect life.

Luxuriate in this feeling of bliss. Embrace this incredible feeling of living your perfect life. And know that you, and only you, have the power to create this life. The life of your vision. The life of your dreams.

As you hold on to this feeling of living your perfect life, slowly become aware of your surroundings and your outside world. When you are ready, open your eyes. Reflect on what you have just envisioned and felt. Now is a good time to jot down some notes in your journal, some key things that came up for you during your life visualization. Think about what you were doing. Were you working? And if so what was your job and profession? Were you in service in any place of your life? And what were the gifts you received? Who were the key people in your life and what were they contributing? What were you contributing to them and to your community? All of this is the beginning of creating your vision.

Your Most Perfect Day:

Next, using the thoughts from this meditative experience that you have written in your journal, allow yourself at least half an hour, and describe in detail the most perfect day (or week) you can possibly imagine. Just start to write and allow your thoughts to flow freely. Use your imagination. Be colorful and descriptive. Include incidents, emotions, and all your senses. Take as much time as you need to describe your most perfect day. *(If necessary, this exercise can be done in a separate sitting, but the sooner you do this after the visualization, the clearer your thoughts will be.)*

Assess Yourself And Discover Your Belief In Having The Life You Love:

You will need your journal again (or the flip chart I mentioned earlier) for these next steps:

Now, let's come back to the present, taking some time to look at your life as it is now. To begin living the life of your vision, it is important that you begin identifying what is working and what is not working in your life now. The purpose of the following exercise is to open up the possibilities for you to believe that living the life you love is now just within reach.

But first, just take a moment to acknowledge yourself for and create a gratitude list in your journal of what is filling you up and giving you joy from the moment you wake to the moment you sleep? What are you grateful for? When are you happiest? What gives you the most pleasure? As you see things in your life change, you can add them to the gratitude pages of your journal.

Now, have some fun with this next exercise. Draw a line down the center of a sheet of paper. You will be creating two lists. Your first list (on the left) will be all the things in your life that you are not happy with; things that you would like to be different. Look at all areas of your life: your family and relationships, job or career, money and finances, energy level, personal development and well-being. What are you tolerating? What don't you like about your life as it is now? What is causing you stress?

Give yourself the gift of some quality time to really look at each one of these items and imagine how each can be different, or better yet, how each might be eliminated. See how each one, if eliminated, would restore a sense of peace and joy, and would clear the way for other possibilities that would get you another step closer to your dreams.

However, if you truly believe any one of these cannot be eliminated or redesigned, you needn't be concerned. You can begin to look at how you can change your attitude so you are at peace and acceptance, and no longer experiencing negative emotion. Remembering your "Attitude of Gratitude," focusing on all you are grateful for, all that is good in your life, will allow you to begin to accept what cannot be changed, and perhaps look at it from a more positive view.

Now on the right side of page, write the second list of how, in the life you love, each item would or could be different. I give you permission to be just a little realistic, but remember, you want to be living your dreams. As you write, allow yourself to look at each of these things and know in your heart that they can happen, that they can be your reality, and that you are the only one who is standing in the way of that happening. Imagine how your life might be different as you go down the list and see how things can change.

Things In My Life I Am Not Happy With:	How Life Would Be Different Without Them:
Example: (Written in past tense as it was and is true for me.)	
My job as a travel agent became boring and draining. I was no longer excited to be working anymore.	Since I have discovered my life purpose is to make a difference in people's lives on a much deeper level, my days are filled with joy and excitement as I coach and build my business.

Values:

In the visualization you experienced earlier in this chapter, your perfect life reflected the relationships, qualities, and/or things that are most important to you. Based on this visualization experience and the description of your perfect day or week, write a list of what you value most in your life. What is most important to you? Are the priorities that you are living now, in the order that you are living them, reflecting those values? Are these the values that you would like to see reflected in your priorities as you create and move toward your life vision and living your dreams?

Writing Your Vision:

Congratulations. You have made it almost to the end of this chapter, this chapter in your life, that is. Your vision is only a crystal ball away. You have explored the true meaning of Vision, Clarity, Passion, and Dreams as it relates to you. You have given yourself the gift of real quality time to spend with yourself (and perhaps a partner in vision) for some deep introspection. You have meditated for perhaps the first time in a long time, or perhaps, maybe the first time ever.

You have already begun to see your future by writing about your most perfect day. You were completely and totally honest with yourself as you rated where you are in your quality of life. You have looked at what is most important to you and how it all reflects in the priorities you live daily. And as we approach the end of this journey, I hope you have made some amazing discoveries about the life you can have.

Now it is time to write your vision. Considering all you have discovered about yourself so far, look into your crystal ball, and what do you see? Begin writing.

Your vision may be as long as you believe necessary, but I suggest you come up with a few words or a couple of sentences that will remind you of the detailed vision. (*You will be able to use your detailed vision to later create your goals, action steps and roadmap to living your dreams.*) This shortened version will help keep you on track as you travel the road to your dreams.

An example of this is my own vision: My vision for my business is quite detailed, over three pages, but the short version is "*I live in my greatness as a Masterful Coach. I have a thriving business and successful coaching practice, living the life of my dreams.*" This reminds me to stay on track if things get a little tough and allows me to always give my clients the best I can possibly give.

Remember, a vision is something you see and feel in your heart that you want to have in your life. When you are connected to your vision, it will guide your actions much like a candle will light your way in the dark. It is not important at this time for you to know how to have it, it is more important that you allow yourself to connect with what is in your heart, and allow it to inspire where you go and what you do in order to turn your vision into reality.

The Final Step:

Stand up and shout your vision to the world. Let the universe hear it. Tell everyone you know. Be accountable to your dreams.

The End:

Or is it really just the beginning?

Your work for now has come to an end. But as we all know, ends are really just beginnings. What is your next step? What will your roadmap look like? What are your short and long term goals? What will your action steps be? Will your action steps lead to fulfilling your goals? What will your life look like in a year? In five years? In ten years? You can break down your life and do the steps in this chapter around specific life areas, like relationship, family, or career.

Begin to create your roadmap by going year by year towards your destination; toward your vision. But please remember; stay open and willing as you may encounter roadblocks. Just know that with your "Attitude of Gratitude," abundance and love, you can get through anything.

Have fun, enjoy the journey, and thank you for trusting not only me, but you.

"*If you can conceive something in your mind and believe it to be true, then you can achieve it.*"—Napoleon Hill

The Right Attitude
Written By Donna M. Krebs

You may have heard the phrase "Attitude is everything." Well, it is. But, more importantly, "Reactions Rule." While attitudes are a state of mind, a reaction to a stimulus, good or bad, has a direct influence on your state of mind. Our reactions are directly tied to what we believe to be true. I'd like to explore with you what truth you believe in and how it dictates the way you react to certain things, situations or events. You'll be surprised how much your reactions rule your life.

When a conflict occurs or something happens to us that doesn't feel good, emotionally, many of us will react negatively. We may get frustrated, angry or even cry causing great distress for ourselves. We actually lose control of our senses. On the other hand, when we experience something wonderful we react with a smile, are usually calm and are very much in control. Deep within each of us is our own unique belief system, taught or impressed upon us at a very young age. A reaction is a switch that is hard wired to our belief system. Reactions, especially those that are toxic to your well being, are the ones I'd like you to be more aware of and how they have no real purpose in your life. Especially, if your have a goal to live a more fulfilling, happier existence.

To demonstrate my point, let's visit something we may all relate to. Someone cuts you off on the parkway. You immediately take the other driver's action personally. You think to yourself, 'They did this to me on purpose!' Even though you don't know this person, you get all worked up and proceed to chase them down the road until you get their attention. Once you have it, you either curse them out or decide to do onto them what they did onto you…you cut them off! These actions could lead to a bigger altercation, a very serious accident or worse. But, unfortunately, you don't take this into consideration before you react and the damage has been done. All you know from the outset is that you've been wronged and you believe that you have to stand up for yourself. The reality is your reaction in this case has no positive outcome for you. And, who wants that? To not react requires a stronger sense of self, an awareness that we all have but seldom use to our advantage. And, awareness is power.

Ok, rewind. You're driving down the parkway, minding your own business, when someone comes up behind you and suddenly gets around you and cuts you off. You pause and become aware that this carelessness is all about them and has nothing to do with you. What a gift you would be giving yourself if you decided to keep your cool, and your distance, instead of pursuing this most inconsiderate person. You see, your awareness kicked in and you took a different path here. To use an old cliché, you took the 'high road' and you made up your mind to let it go instead of engaging. You've saved yourself from an unknown aggravation and down time plus you're getting to your destination in one piece. I'm not suggesting that you become a pacifist, far from it. This was an example of either becoming a road-rage recruit or being a person with awareness, clarity and control. Empower yourself with a healthy response. The message here is to let go of the things that do not warrant any unnecessary attention or action. Clearly, if this driver is creating a hazard on the road and poses a danger, try to get his or her license plate, pull your car over and call the highway police. They will handle the situation appropriately. It will serve you best to respond in a level-headed, responsible manner instead of reacting with your emotions.

Discovery Through Awareness:

So, how do you go about obtaining more awareness to think clearly, especially when suddenly confronted with a negative situation that doesn't feel right? Try asking yourself this simple question each and every time: 'By reacting in a hostile or emotional manner, will my actions make me feel better in the end or influence the situation to have a better overall outcome?' The answer will almost always certainly be 'Not really.' Getting control of a bad reaction before it manifests into something nasty or ugly takes discipline, because as I mentioned earlier, you need to have a greater awareness of yourself. Remember the old saying "When you get mad, slowly count to ten before you say or do anything?" Well, try it. By slowly counting to ten, you're releasing the steam of the reaction and allowing yourself to 1) calm down 2) realize what's really going on and 3) formulating a proper response to the situation at hand. To practice awareness, my suggestion is to replay any recent occurrences in your life where you reacted negatively, especially badly. Play the scene over in your mind, but replace all the negativity with positive images or responses. If you want it, you can visualize it and you can live it. Pause at every crucial moment to allow yourself the opportunity to become more aware of what's going on around you. By pausing, you're giving yourself the gift of awareness and you will know how to respond appropriately to any given situation.

Here's an example, I went into a convenience store to buy milk. I pick up a brand that appeared to be on sale having a reduced price sign in front of it. When I brought it up to the cashier, she rang up the full price instead of the sale price. I became aware that she didn't know that there was a sale sign in front of the milk and, rather than react badly to the fact that I was about to be overcharged, I said with a calm voice, "I believe the milk is on sale because there appeared to be a sign in front of it." She looked at me like I had six noses and politely asked that I show her. When I walked her over to the case, she pointed out that the sign was for the eggs, instead of the milk, that were right next to it. I agreed and said 'Oh well, it looked as if it were for the milk.' As we walked back to the counter, I was prepared to pay more for the milk but then she said, "Because you're so kind about it, I'll give you the milk for the sale price of the eggs." That was really a moment for me and I thanked her graciously. She explained that most times she encounters very irate people and it's always nice to work with people who can be civil. The experience inspired me to be more gracious under fire.

Deep Dive:

Now, let's kick it up a notch. I just described how to thwart negative reactions. By doing so, I influenced a positive outcome without trying. But more importantly, I let go of my need to be right. We all have it, this need to be right. True needs are non-negotiable. Our real need for water, air and love cannot be traded for anything. While we can't convert these for other needs, we can realistically let go of our deep seeded need to be right in everyone's eyes. We can convert our need to be right into a need to live a happier, more carefree life filled with inner peace and solace. Ask yourself, what does it really matter? The most important thing to remember is that you know that you're right and you can sleep at night hanging your hat on this truth.

I find myself letting go of my need to be right each and every day. For instance, the other day I met up with another car coming from a different direction at a four-way stop sign but we're both now headed in the same direction. Who, lawfully, should move forward first? The car with the 'Right of Way' does. Meaning, if the car is to your right, they go first. But, no one uses this rule. So, even though the car was to my left, I smiled and waved them on. I let go of my need to be right and there was a healthier outcome. I'm happy, they're happy and we're all moving forward.

The Truth About Interpretations:

Put two people in the same situation, and, more times than not, both will walk away with a different interpretation of what they have just experienced. It makes sense because each one of us processes information differently. People will also typically form opinions based on assumptions and hearsay (other's interpretations). Once those opinions are created, they become the "truth" and to convince you otherwise becomes an uphill battle. Anxiety and anguish caused by this conflict can drain you of your energy and leave you frustrated. So, is it really worth your mental health to fret over the fact that someone's interpretation is different from yours? Give yourself permission to let it go and the real truth will eventually float to the surface for all to see.

I recently faced such a situation. I'm a Project Manager for a well-known organization and my department hit some tough times last year. Several senior managers were terminated and corporate decided to bring in someone to 'clean-house.' A new Director transferred over to our group and I was now reporting to him. I was told that things were a mess and that he had to make some serious changes. Instead of starting with a clean slate and forming opinions based on his own experience, he chose to listen to the interpretations of the very people who were at the root cause of the problems within the department. He formulated some terrible assumptions using this information. One of them, unfortunately, was about me. Even though I'm a professional Project Manager whose job it is to direct production support associates and hold them accountable for their tasks due to the strict driven deadlines given to us by the business owners, I was accused of being difficult, unapproachable, and autocratic. Instead of supporting me, and the role that I was hired to do, he proceeded to tell me that I was wrong in thinking that I was the "Queen" and needed corrective action. I spent hours trying to prove to him that I was doing a conscientious job, protecting company revenue, and creating new and appropriate processes that produced a more efficient method of working between the various groups. I was a dedicated employee who had focus and purpose. He needed to realize that the people we were supporting took every opportunity to make the department look bad instead of doing their part and collaborating with us, as they needed to do. But, after hitting a brick wall with his attitude, I realized that I needed to just let go of my need to be right. All of my explaining was not going to change his interpretation of me, or the situation, no matter how hard I tried to plead my case. So, after I gained a greater awareness that I was unable to change things, I just let it go. I knew I had the power of choice and I made a serious decision to leave the company. They had provided me with a job, but I'm in control of my career after all. Plus, I wanted to be where I was celebrated instead of tolerated.

By my letting go of my need to be right, my energy took a different path. The anxiety that I was experiencing prior to my 'letting go' experience turned into an even more intense focus and drive. Rather than compete for acceptance, I created an environment where I was hard to resist. In three short months, I went from an employee on notice to an employee of the month! And, on the very day I was given the award by the General Manager/Executive VP of the company, I received a phone call for a job interview. I was able to attract what I wanted to by believing in myself. The manager who originally had doubts about me saw me for who I truly am; a person of integrity and reliability. I didn't tell him this fact. He experienced it for himself. He now knows he can count on me to help him and his department succeed. My name is carved on a plaque in the lobby where I work and it makes me proud. Every time I see my name in brass I'm reminded of how I overcame adversity just by letting go of my need to be right at that moment, being aware of who I am and creating a better overall outcome for myself.

Other Courses Of Action:

Most managers respond well to proactive dialog, conversations initiated by you. If your job performance is in question talking to your manager or supervisor about it will bring things into focus so that you'll at least know where you stand. Once you've identified where the gaps are you'll be in a better position to close them or at least make them smaller. If your manager is stubborn or unapproachable meet with the Human Resources manager and express your concerns. Frame your thoughts in a way that will attract them to you. Stating, for example, "I really enjoy working for this company and I'd like remain here and continue to contribute to its growth to the best of my ability" clearly says you care about the company and want to continue to be a part of it in a positive way. Adding, "I feel there are areas where I can improve and it would be beneficial to me if you can help me to identify these areas so that I can work on them right away" shows that you realize something is awry and you're willing to address it head-on. You'll be tempted to defend yourself if you receive negative feedback on your performance, but resist the urge. The feedback reflects how they view and interpret you. Request that a development plan be created on your behalf so that you can actively tackle the areas where you appear to be weak. Your manager has to communicate and manage your expectations as far as what they want from you on the job and in turn you have to manage their expectations. It's perfectly ok to request a job description to review the responsibilities of the job. Sometimes they're updated and no one knows about it except the Human Resources manager. Meet with them or your manager regularly to evaluate your performance against the plan. Come your review time there should be no surprises.

Another insight that I brought to the surface during my personal trial and tribulation was that I realized that I didn't need others to validate who I am or what I'm worth. Truth be told, they are not my maker. I held onto that belief and it fueled me onto greater things and an even happier self. You can achieve the same but only if you decide to let go of the things you can't change, whether it's a careless action on someone's part or a sorted opinion. Fuel the things you can and want to change. It's all about you and what's inside of you that matters most. This may require a shift in your current thinking.

Exercise:

Periodically, it's always good to assess and evaluate how healthy you are, what you believe in, what you stand for, what you care about and what you want for yourself tomorrow, next week, next month and even next year. By assessing yourself and identifying the areas that may need improving, you are also strengthening your own personal awareness for what you truly want out of life. To help you, fill in the following chart. For each question, provide an honest personal assessment of yourself and provide an objective and a plan for improvement for each. Be creative but keep it simple. With some questions you may think there is no room for improvement or it's futile to improve. Close your eyes, take a deep breath, and open your mind to what's possible. Evaluate your answers now and from time to time so you can fine tune them along the way. By writing down your personal assessment, objectives & plan you've actually created a path for self-improvement. By committing your thoughts to paper, by way of this chart, you will be more likely to move forward with action and realize positive changes in your life. You will clearly observe your own personal growth and it will continually fuel you to achieve more.

Date: _____

Topic	Question	Assessment	Objective	Plan
Health/Well Being	On a scale of 1 to 10 (10 being the best), how healthy am I today physically?	*Example:* 5	*Example:* I would like to rate an 8 in two months. I want to lose 10 lbs.	*Example:* Briskly walk 20 minutes everyday at lunchtime. Eliminate snacks after 7:00 PM.
	Do I want to be healthier?	*Example:* Yes	*Example:* I want to glow	*Example:* Drink more water in a day & smile at everyone you see.
	On a scale of 1 to 10 (10 being the best), how healthy am I emotionally?			
	Can I be happier?			
	On a scale of 1 to 10 (10 being the best), how attractive am I?			
	Do I want to be more attractive?			
Beliefs	What do I like about myself?			
	Do I want to enrich or strengthen the things I like about myself?			
	What do I dislike about myself?			
	Do I care enough to change the things that I dislike about myself?			
	Who do I want to emulate?			
	Who are my friends?			
	Who do I trust most?			
	Who can I go to in a time of need for support?			
	Do I permit my family to influence my life and the decisions that I make?			

Topic	Question	Assessment	Objective	Plan
Convictions	What is the single most important issue for me today?			
	Do I want to have a positive influence on others?			
	How can I honestly be a better person?			
Planning	What do I want to do tomorrow?			
	What do I want to accomplish by next week?			
	What do I want to achieve by next month?			
	Six months from now, where do I want to be in my life?			
	One year from now, what one goal do I want to reach personally and			

Parting Thoughts:

By "tuning in" to yourself, you create a greater awareness of who you are and what your beliefs are. Maintaining the chart and evaluating yourself periodically (at least once a month) will help you to grow a stronger sense of self. The stronger you are the more positive influences you will be able to create and attract.

I hope I've given you some yummy food for thought or at least some seeds that you can start to grow fruitful things with. Remember, "Reactions Rule" and they reveal who you really are, your true colors. What do your reactions say about you?

Seven Steps To Create Lasting Positive Change In Your Life
Written By Lisa Jaworowski

I must confess up front: I am a self-help junkie. That's right, for as long as I can remember, I have been obsessed with this topic. My "habit" started in my teen years, thumbing through my father's well-worn copy of Dr. Norman Vincent Peale's *The Power of Positive Thinking*. I moved on to listening to Wayne Dyer audiotapes, and then to books like *Chicken Soup for the Soul*, Deepak Chopra's *Spiritual Laws for Success*, the works of Tony Robbins, Steven Covey, and recently Dr. Phil. To this day, I am always ready for new insights on self-improvement.

Fortunately, it seems that I am not alone in my addiction. I recently did a search for self-help books online with a major bookstore, and I was overwhelmed to find over 61,000 titles in this subject. That's pretty impressive, isn't it? So it appears that countless other individuals today are also enthusiastically searching for "something more" in their lives.

It seems inevitable that with these interests I would pursue a career related to this field; first as a certified psychotherapist, and currently as a personal development and career coach. My own life has been an ongoing process of change and "reinventing" myself over the years. I strongly believe that we must keep growing throughout our lives.

One important concept that I have learned to embrace, is the idea that feeling unsettled or dissatisfied is not necessarily a bad way to feel. It is just a sign, that it may be time to make some changes in your life. As Wayne Dyer states in *The Power of Intention*, we must all learn to "feel complete with our incomplete selves", something we do not consciously think about doing or acknowledge while we are in the midst of change. Simple words, simple concepts, yes? But, as we all know, not that simple to accept and implement.

So, after you have acknowledged your desire to grow, how do you sort through all the self-help information available today? Where do you start the process of actually using some of this advice in your own daily life?

I have put together a list of what I believe are seven of the most important steps to follow if you want to move forward in your life. These are the steps that are utilized most frequently in my research, training, and experience over the years as I have read countless books and listened to dozens of audiotapes on self-improvement. They are also the methods followed by those people who have successfully made lasting and positive changes in their lives.

Below you will find a brief outline of these seven steps.They are the steps that I have used in my personal development workshops and individual coaching sessions. They form the core of my coaching programs for every aspect of personal success. What follows in this chapter is an introduction to each of these concepts along with some examples, questions and guidelines that will help you understand how you can incorporate each of these steps into your personal success plan.

Here are the seven steps. As you read this chapter, I suggest you follow the sequence of the steps as outlined below. Work at your own pace and allow yourself enough time to complete the writing exercises that accompany each step.

1. Accept that you are accountable for all that happens in your life.
2. Clearly and specifically define what you want to change.
3. Ask yourself why you want to change and what it actually means to you.
4. Set reasonable and realistic priorities and time limits.
5. Break your goals down into small, simple steps.
6. Take some type of action on at least one of your goals every single day.
7. Frequently review, reevaluate and redirect your actions.

As you read this chapter, I also suggest that you use either a notebook or journal to record your answers to the questions and your personal thoughts on each step. I have found writing to be a very powerful tool in coaching for success. Dreams and goals become more "real" when you write them down. Writing also allows you to review your plans frequently for inspiration and to formally acknowledge your accomplishments.

Step #1: Accept And Acknowledge That You Are Accountable For All That Happens In You Life.

This step must be the first concept you grasp on your self improvement journey. As Dr. Phil says, "You either get it or you don't." It is the "good news, bad news" story. The "good news" is that is all up to you. The "bad news" is that it is all up to you. No way out.

So what does being accountable really mean? It means that you realize that in any situation you always have a choice as to how you respond to each situation. You cannot control the actions of others, but you can always control your own response to those actions. By acknowledging this concept, you accept the fact that you cannot blame anyone else for the problems that exist in your life:

Your past does not predict your future.

You cannot change the past, only the hold that it has on you.

How often have we read the success stories of those with seemingly impossible obstacles to overcome? These people are the individuals who have chosen not to blame their surroundings or their circumstances and have taken control of their own possibilities and moved forward in their lives.

Each and every one of us has this same opportunity, if we choose to accept it.

Consider "Karen's" case (fictitious name). Karen was very dissatisfied with the direction her life seemed to be going in. Karen was the mother of two active, elementary school age boys, and the wife of a hard working, somewhat "demanding" husband. She lived in a modest sized home in a nice suburban area. Karen had always felt that she possessed quite a bit of artistic ability and for many years she had wanted to pursue a career in a related field. Now that her youngest son was in school full-time, she thought it would be the ideal time to resurrect these dreams.

However, Karen also had a long list of reasons why she felt it might not be possible for her to pursue her goals. She wanted to be home for the boys when they got home from school in the afternoon. During the day while they were at school she said she needed to run errands and clean the house. She worried what would happen if one of them got sick during the day at school and needed her. If she waited until the evenings or weekends to go out, she felt that she didn't want to burden her husband with "babysitting". But, then on the other hand, if he did agree to help out, she wondered would he be able to take care of them properly according to her high standards of child care.

I asked Karen to imagine that all these problems had "magically" been solved, and they no longer existed. Would she then be able to move forward? Was there anything else that might stop her from taking action? After doing this exercise and spending some time being very introspective, Karen admitted that one of the main reasons she had not yet been able to try anything new was because she had some serious doubts about her own artistic abilities. It had been a long time since she had felt creative and she was afraid of failure.

Together, after several coaching sessions, we came up with a plan that would allow Karen to "test the waters" in the art field as well as allow her to fulfill her obligations as a mother and a wife. Her first, small step was to enroll in a one hour painting class in the evening at a local craft store. She chose a class that was offered at the same time that her husband could take her sons to their weekly sports practice session. When the class was over, she decided to try an online art class that she could conveniently complete at home. After she had completed these two "test" classes, she felt confident enough to start taking art courses at the local community college.

Karen's case helps to illustrate this concept of accountability. We all often have busy and demanding lives to deal with. We have obligations to family members and hectic social schedules. However, most often the biggest obstacle to making changes in our lives is our own limiting belief system. When we learn to put aside our excuses and be honest with ourselves, we can always find a way, however small, to take a step forward.

In my opinion, that is definitely the good news—it's all up to you!

Step #2: Clearly And Specifically Define What You Want To Change.

Before you start out on any journey, the first thing that you usually do is decide upon a destination, right? You think about where you are going and what it will be like when you get there.

The same principles hold true for this journey. You should try to be imaginative and let yourself dream. Why not? We will look at your specific goals more closely later, but for now just work on visualizing the way your life will look when you have achieved some of your dreams and goals. What are some of the things you will be doing, saying, feeling? What pictures come to mind? Where will you be?

I often guide my clients to think about dividing their goals into three life areas.

Individual, personal goals. These goals would include changes you want to make in your physical health as well your emotional health such as improving your diet, exercising more and reducing stress.

Relationship, family goals. Some examples of these goals are improving communications, spending more time with family members or perhaps eliminating negative relationships in your life.

Career, financial goals. These two sets of goals often go together as they may include changing jobs, returning to college or starting your own business.

Here is an exercise that will help you start to clarify and visualize your personal goals.

I.   Using the guidelines I just discussed, make a list of the things that you want to change in your life. List as many as you like in any of the three areas.

Individual and Personal Goals:

a)

b)

c)

d)

e)

Relationship and Family Goals:

a)

b)

c)

d)

e)

Career and Financial Goals:

a)

b)

c)

d)

e)

II. Think about how your life will be different after you have made these changes? Describe what you will be doing and how you will feel. Create a powerful visual image of this "new, improved" you that you can easily bring to the forefront of your mind to help keep you focused on your goals. Use the space provided to write as many details about your vision that comes into your mind.

III. What will be the first sign that change is beginning? When you notice that first change, what can you do to keep the ball rolling?

Signs of Change:

Ways to Maintain the Changes:

Step #3: The Reasons Behind Your Goals.

Ask yourself why you want to change and what it actually means to you.

After creating your list of goals, it is also very important to spend some time reflecting on the reasons behind these goals. The purpose behind your goals is a very strong motivating force. If your desire to achieve something is strong and sincere you will almost certainly find a way to accomplish it.

Take a look at each of your goals and ask yourself the following questions. Use the space below each question to record your thoughts.

I.   "Why do I want this? What do I hope to achieve if I reach this goal?"

Expand on the visualization exercise in Step Two and imagine what your life will be like if you succeed. Is the end result what you were hoping for?

II.   "What will this goal do for the quality of my emotional self?"

Individuals often set monetary or materialistic goals thinking that after they acquire these things they will feel a certain way; and then are frequently disappointed when these new acquisitions do not improve their self-esteem or self-confidence. Of course, it is absolutely acceptable to have goals that include becoming more successful financially or acquiring possessions, as long as you are clear about the end result and keep your expectations realistic.

III.   "How has my desire to achieve this goal been influenced by other people in my life? Am I doing this to please someone else besides myself? Parents? Spouse?"

If your primary reasons for achieving a goal are really those of someone else, your success will be limited and emotionally unfulfilling. You need to learn to tune out the "static" of other people's needs and wants to be able to focus on what is truly in your own heart and mind.

IV. "Is this a temporary goal, or one that I will be committed to for the long haul?"

We have all made those New Year's resolutions or tried to lose weight to look better for that special occasion. But, what happens after the event is over and the New Year gets older? Goals that are directed towards healthy and positive life changes are more empowering than short term goals with a limited purpose.

Step #4: Establish Priorities And Realistic Time Limits.

Now that you have listed your goals and reasons, you need to identify your top priority goals and decide upon the time within which you are committed to accomplishing them. While you are doing this you will need to keep in mind your own unique circumstances including family obligations, financial issues and anything else that will influence your course of action. For example, Karen spoke about her dream to use her artistic talents to become an art teacher; but she realized that this would have to be a long term goal due to her family obligations and financial restrictions at the time.

Look at your complete list of goals in all three areas from Step Two and think about the timeframe in which you hope to achieve this goal. I usually have my clients break down their goals into three time periods. Assign each goal a time limit according to the following guidelines and write it next to the goal.

1. Immediate goals—these are the goals that you're ready to start working on today.
2. Short term goals—goals that you hope to accomplish within the next few months.
3. Long term goals—these are goals that will take a year or several years to achieve.

To break this list down even further; in each of the three life areas described in Step Two, identify your top three goals. You can identify fewer than three; but, I do not recommend starting with more than three goals in each area. Too many goals can be overwhelming at first when creating your specific action plans. We will save the others for future use after you achieve your top priority ones. Keep this complete list of goals and review it often, it will help keep you inspired for the future.

Top Three Individual and Personal Goals/Immediate, Short, or Long Term

1.

2.

3.

Top Three Relationship and Family Goals/Immediate, Short or Long Term

1.

2.

3.

Top Three Career and Financial Goals/Immediate, Short or Long Term

1.

2.

3.

You should now have revised lists divided into the three life categories (individual or personal goals, relationship or family goals, and career or financial goals), your top three goals in each area and the time limit you have assigned to each of those goals. These are the lists that we will take to the next step.

Step #5: Break Your Goals Down Into Small, Simple Steps.

The directions are short and simple, but yet they are one of the most important in goal setting. This is the step that some people feel they can skip over after they have repeatedly reviewed their goals in the previous steps. But, this is most definitely not the case. Goals need to be broken down into the smallest steps possible so that it will be easy to decide what you need to do each day. A detailed list also offers you choices to match your time limits and physical and emotional energy levels.

Choose one of your top priority and immediate goals to work on first. For example, one of "Karen's" personal top priority and immediate goals included her desire to "take an art class". At first glance, this goal may seem specific, but it is actually too vague. In order to create a clear action plan, this goal had to be broken down into much smaller steps.

When looking at your goals, you ask yourself, "What skills, abilities, beliefs, and knowledge do I need to achieve this goal?"

Karen's list of specific steps towards taking an art class included the following steps:

I.   Research art classes offered in the area and start a notebook with the information obtained.

    a.   Go online to browse college course catalogs
    b.   Look in local yellow pages under Art Classes
    c.   Call friend from PTA with similar interests
    d.   Read local newspaper ads
    e.   Call school district Adult Education office

II. Make necessary phone calls—this step was broken down even further as Karen obtained more information, including phone numbers and days and times to call key contact people.

III. Choose a class that fits in with family schedule and personal comfort level.

IV. Discuss options with family, ask for their support.

V.   Register for the class.

VI. Attend class!

Step #6: Take Action On At Least One Of Your Goals Every Single Day.

Begin each day with the question "What can I do today to make my life better?"

For years, I have been printing out "business" cards with my favorite quotes on them for my clients to tape on their mirrors or keep in their pocket.I also keep a separate page on my website for the same purpose. The card with the quote above is one of the most popular ones. The importance of this step cannot be understated.

Every journey begins with a single step.

After you have created your detailed list in Step Five, you should review it daily and decide what action you will take that day towards reaching one of your goals. The action you decide to take does not need to be a big one, the important concept is that you must get yourself into the daily habit of taking at least one action, no matter how small.

Steps I can take today towards one or more of my goals:

1.

2.

3.

These small steps add up very quickly, and any small step is certainly better than no step at all, right? One small step each day of the week would add up to 7 actions for that week, times 4 weeks equals 28 steps, and so on. Do you see how quickly one small step each day can move you towards your goal? Most of our short term goals require fewer than 28 steps to reach completion; look at Karen's list in Step Five.

Your smallest step can be as simple as looking up one phone number online or in the phone book and then just writing it down in your notebook. If you don't have the time to make the call that same day, then you have the number ready and waiting for your next step. However, chances are, once you make the decision to take one step, you will do more and the momentum builds.

If you follow this daily action process, within one month you could easily achieve a small goal. Imagine how you will feel in just one month if you commit to this plan.

Step #7: Review, Reevaluate, and Redirect.

It is very important to evaluate your plan often to make sure your action steps are working for you the way you have intended.

In *First Things First*, author Stephen Covey advises individuals to review goals and priorities often to be sure that you have your "ladder leaning against the right wall". You would not want to get all the way to the top and then find out that you have been climbing the wrong wall.

I also ask clients to imagine how they will feel in a month from now if they did nothing towards working on their goals. Although, I always try to keep clients focused in a positive direction during coaching, I find this exercise can be useful in sustaining motivation. Tony Robbins speaks of this as the "Pain vs. Pleasure principle".

What will it cost you if you do not take action now?

If you find that you are not moving forward, you will need to do some "trouble shooting" to see where you may be getting stuck.

Are you breaking down your goals into small enough steps?

Are your goals realistic for your current life situation?

Are there people in your life who are resistant to the changes you are trying to make or who may be "sabotaging" your plans?

Are there any personal "blocks" keeping you from success? What are your own limiting beliefs?

One Final Step.

Although I have left this step for the end, it is a step that can be done simultaneously with each of the seven steps mentioned above. It is a step that most people leave out entirely, although it is a simple one.

Be sure to give yourself credit for each and every step you complete.

Most individuals do not feel comfortable patting themselves on the back for fear of appearing conceited or full of themselves. This self praise can be a very private matter. Whatever your method, just be sure you do not skip this step. Take the time to browse through your journal or notebook and focus on what you have achieved so far,.

Change can be a difficult process, but the results are well worth the time and energy you put into the process.

In *Simple Abundance,* Sarah Ban Breathnach encourages us to:

"Be patient toward all that is unsolved in your heart and try to love the questions themselves. We need to learn to live the questions, and become open to the changes that the answers will inevitably bring."

After all,

"You only live once—but if you work it right, once is enough."—Joe E. Lewis

Chapter Three:
Building Extraordinary Relationships

Creating Harmonious Relationships
Written By Bonnie R. Schizzano

Curious about how you can improve some of the relationships in your life? Good for you! Whether these relationships are with family, friends, or colleagues, help is on the way. Since you are the common denominator in all these relationships, you are already in a position to make change happen.

Begin by thinking about why it is important for you to create and maintain harmonious relationships. Becoming aware of reasons for enhancing your relationships is a good first step toward change. Here are some possibilities to consider. Place a check mark next to those that you identify with.

1. Greater peace of mind
2. Deeper connection and camaraderie with others
3. Increased intimacy
4. Bringing out the best in yourself and others
5. More fun and laughter
6. Improved health
7. Greater enjoyment

Now that you are aware of these ideas, ask yourself what *is* preventing you from having greater harmony in your relationships? Sometimes there are barriers right at the beginning of a relationship. Other times, barriers seem to creep into a relationship when no one is looking. It is not surprising that people, even people with whom you are very close, think differently than you do. What is surprising is how great the differences can be and how they can result in disharmony. My intention is to explore with you that which creates the great diversity in how individuals process information and to provide opportunities for you to learn to improve your responses to people who play a role in your life.

Are you familiar with Anthony Robbins? He is often described as a motivational guru, but I like to call him an "empowerment junkie." Yes, he motivates and uses motivation as a tool for gaining greater power in life. He has certainly empowered himself to worldwide fame and fortune. He uses an exercise, similar to the one that follows, to demonstrate a common misconception that everyone experiences the same reality. You will find that all perception is subjective and has a direct impact on how you think about things. That is why people often have entirely different interpretations of identical situations. This simple, but effective, exercise will give you insight into how this works:

1. Think about the color blue
2. Look carefully around the room or your environment
3. Notice everything that is blue
4. Find as much blue as you can in 30 seconds
5. Make a mental note of everything that is blue

Make sure you stop and do this exercise right now, so that you experience this process before moving on.

6. Now that you have identified everything that is blue, without looking around further
7. Name all the things that are orange in the room

After scanning for everything that is colored blue, what happened when you tried to find things that are orange? Very often, people have little, if any, awareness of seeing any orange objects, and are quite surprised to find all the orange that is there, once they begin to look for it. Was that your experience? It is also quite interesting to realize just how much blue is noticed when focusing intensely. This exercise tells you what to look for, specifically, when it asks you to look for the color blue. In reality, every individual possesses their own unique *color*, made up of their history, personality and life experiences. It only takes a slight variation in *color* to influence what will or will not be observed. How can knowing this serve to your advantage? How can it make you more tolerant of others?

"What we see depends mainly on what we look for."—Sir John Lubbock, source unknown

There is a saying that comes out of the field of Neuro Linguistic Programming, which is; *The Map is Not the Territory.* If you are not familiar with Neuro

Linguistic Programming, or NLP for short, it is a model that was developed in the 1970's that teaches the *how* in creating excellent results, based on effective communication, personal change, and greater enjoyment of life. NLP's guiding principles are referred to as pre-suppositions, one of which is, as previously stated, *The Map is Not the Territory.* Another way to say this can be *The Menu is Not the Meal.* The meal is represented on the menu, just as the territory is represented on the map. To take this one step further, think about your life and your understanding of reality. You cannot know reality without having an influence on it. In the exercise of looking for the color blue, your observation for the color blue passed through your filter and, in so doing, you deleted all other colors. Everything you experience is through your filters. These filters are made up of your history, beliefs, values, decisions and desires. If you were to turn your use of filters into a presupposition, you could say, *Your Living Experience is Your Reality.* Another way to say this is, *The Experience You are Having is YourModel of the World.*

Shelle Rose Charvet is a worldwide Trainer of one particular aspect of NLP called Meta Programs. Similar to the software in a computer, Meta Programs are internal programs that serve as filters to how you interact with the world. They help to explain, in detail, the many differences in a person's basic thought processes. For example, are you aware that there are many different factors that influence how you become and stay motivated? Ask yourself, in relation to your work, how do I know I have done a good job? Responses can vary from something like, "Someone told me I have done a good job" to "I just know." How would you answer this question? Studies show that in the work context, 40% of the population has an external frame that needs to be told they have done a good job in order for them to *know* they have. Another 40% of the population has an internal frame that automatically assumes they have done a good job, and does not need any external reinforcement. The remaining 20% of the population has both external and internal frames, which means they sense when they have done a good job but they also seek external acknowledgment. This is only one out of a number of questions that will tell you something about motivation, which is always unique in its context and is a representation of the different ways in which people process information and experience various situations that occur. Are you beginning to understand the different needs people have that are attributed to their internal programs?

In the beginning of many of her workshops, Shelley Rose Charvet points to a small spot on the floor, that she names "Reality." When she wants to have a "reality check" to make a point, she refers to that location, because she knows a pure "Reality" does not really exist; that it is the way you perceive and interpret it, through *your model of the world.*

"We don't see things as they are. We see them as we are."—Anais Nin, author of *The Diary of Anais Nin*

In 1957, Noam Chomsky came up with three processes that are used by people for filtering information. These three processes are known as deletion, distortion, and generalization and are part of the basic communication model used in NLP. The process of deletion allows us to selectively take in and absorb what is important or meaningful to us and then delete all other information that we do not perceive as important. Have you had the experience of becoming interested in something, such as a specific car or a particular style of house? Suddenly, you begin to see that car or that house everywhere you go. That is because you engaged certain filters so that you are now filtering for those specific things. The process of distortion is your imagination at work. You use distortion to think about, create, and change things all the time. Have you ever imagined what a room would look like painted a certain color or with furniture arranged in a particular way? Have you ever projected something happening in the future? Distortion provides you with the ability to do this. The third process of generalization enables you to turn an example into a general principle. This is incredibly helpful in one's ability to learn a particular skill, such as opening a door, and then translate that skill into the ability to open all kinds of different doors. It is through generalization that you develop your principles and beliefs. Just as a coin has two different sides, your filters are also different and, therefore, can aid or hinder you, depending on how they were formed.

"We don't need more strength or more ability or greater opportunity. What we need is to use what we have."—Basil S. Walsh

With the ability to delete, distort and generalize, you directly and unconsciously impact your reality at its deepest level. Now that you have an awareness of filters, you can begin to focus your attention more closely on the role they play, particularly with respect to your relationships. When you find you are anticipating, imagining, or expecting something in advance, you are, in all likelihood, operating on "automatic filter." If your encounters with others are not how you would like them to be—then it is time to either change or adjust your filters.

Try taking some of the following actions, and notice how changing your responses also change the responses of others.

1. Do something kind for someone who would never expect it.

    For whom will you do this?

    What act of kindness will you do?

2. Offer a challenging person the benefit of the doubt.

    Who is your best choice?

    Why?

3. Provide someone space to "act out," and do not take it personally.

    To whom will you provide this opportunity?

4. Create a new positive belief about yourself and act as if it is true.

    What is the empowering belief you will embrace about yourself today?

5. Look for a positive quality in someone and tell him or her about it.

    What are a few positive qualities to choose from to tell them?

6. Plan for things to start going your way over the next three months and see what happens. If you think there are certain things in your life that are not going your way, begin to think, act and talk as if they are going your way.

    What specific things in your life are going your way now?

    How, exactly, are they going your way?

7. Make positive statements about someone and share it with others.

    Who will benefit from this act of kindness?

Now, can you understand that you see things, not necessarily as they are, but as you want them to be, through *your model of the world*? Likewise, your loved ones, your friends and your colleagues also see things through *their model of the world*. The opportunity to embrace diversity and share differences is truly a refreshing one. So, what is preventing you from experiencing more balance and harmony?

"A monk was once asked, 'What do you do there in the monastery?' He replied, 'We fall and get up, fall and get up, fall and get up again.'" Tito Colliander, spiritual guide and author of *Way of the Ascetics*

A major factor that contributes to strife and creates disharmony in relationships, is the principle of wanting to be right. Do you notice a preoccupation for people, possibly even yourself at times, to insist on being right? But right according to whom? A statement is made but something different is understood. Two people remember the same thing in two entirely differently ways. Something happens and is never to be forgotten or forgiven. What price have you paid in your quest to be right?

What is so important about being right, anyway? Have you ever tried to prove that you are right, to the point where you became obsessed with being right? Perhaps at some level, certain needs are driving that determined behavior. Recognizing that such behavior may be an attempt to meet a particular need can provide you with greater understanding of the source of your actions. It will take humility to answer these questions honestly and make changes that will enable you to replace righteousness with happiness.

Ask yourself if being right could, somehow, fulfill any of these needs:

1. Does it give me a sense of security?

2. Does it give me a feeling of control?

3. Is it how I get my way?

4. Does it give me a sense of autonomy?

5. Does it give me a feeling of power?

6. Does it give me a sense of independence?

7.   Is it a way of getting my needs met?

It is important to truly understand how you want things to be, because sometimes confusion causes you to lose focus about what it is that you are really trying to accomplish. First, imagine that all of your needs have already been met. Inside, you are feeling secure with a sense of independence, autonomy, and control. You know how to compromise and still have your needs fulfilled. Therefore, it is no longer necessary for you to insist on having your way. You have mastered the art of inner fitness. How do you feel, now? Do you feel more accepting and peaceful? Do you find that there is no more driving force to be right? Could it be that the truth about being right is similar to what is said about happiness, i.e., "Happiness is an inside job"?

There might be a whole other way to go about this. The harmonious relationships that you are seeking might be the very thing—the more holistic way—to also meet your needs. As you allow yourself to be more accepting and understanding, more open to others and less judgmental, you enhance that quality in yourself. You find that as you build deeper connections in your relationships, you fill the same needs in yourself. You can toss that "wanting to be right" behavior out the window. As your relationships become more fun, sincere, and harmonious—so do you.

"How many cares one loses when one decides not to be something, but to be someone."
—Coco Chanel, Entrepreneur & Fashion Designer

There is a universal principle called the "law of attraction" that is receiving a great deal of attention. Have you ever heard of it? It is based on the vibration of your feelings and claims that whatever you are feeling you are attracting to yourself. "Like" attracts "Like." You can imagine that the "law of attraction" is a tremendous motivator for letting go of annoying and bothersome feelings and replacing them with positive and pleasurable ones. The bottom line is that you are actually manifesting the very things that you are focusing on, that you do *and* do not want. At first this may seem like a lot for you to digest and can be especially "tricky" because pointing a finger at someone else is always easier or more easily justified. Regardless of the level of energy, what matters for you are *your* reactions and *your* focus because that is what you ultimately *attract* to yourself.

If you want to feel good and attract the things you want into your life, consider the following:

1. Who do you blame and why?

    State your reasons and, instead of blame, offer understanding.

2. In what instances and with whom do you sense incompleteness?

    Provide an explanation for what seems to be incomplete for each person.

    Now, be complete.

3. When and with whom are you annoyed?

    What are some positive thoughts and actions you can take to free yourself from negative reactions?

4. Do you find yourself thinking about what you do not want, over and over again?

Describe in detail what you do want. How does it look, sound, feel, and taste?

Keep thinking about what you want now, over and over again. Write it down.

5. Do you get angry with others?

Find three ways to have compassion.

1.

2.

3.

6. Are you resentful toward others?

What are three things you would say to a child who had resentment toward a friend?

1.

2.

3.

7. Do you experience times of despair? When?

What are the hopes you are afraid to hope for?

1.

2.

3.

Because each person's life is defined by *their own model of the world*, it is very probable that you do not understand many of the reactions of other people. Can you imagine the resourceful state and positive feelings you could create for yourself and others by attracting the kind of energy that could be a result of responding favorably to any of the previous ideas? The "law of attraction" guarantees that you will receive whatever you *feel* at the energetic level. You will begin to notice more wonderful possibilities in your relationships when you apply the principles of the "law of attraction."

"The weak can never forgive. Forgiveness is an attribute of the strong."
—Mahatma Gandhi

In the 1960's, Jose Silva developed a system that is considered to be a landmark in the study of human consciousness. Today this system is called the Silva Ultramind ESP System. It is based on the principle of unlocking the power of your mind and learning to intuit information to create a successful, happy, and fulfilled life.

Originally, Jose Silva set out to help his children improve their performance in school. He used a theory from his knowledge of electronics, of lowering resistance to increase receptivity. He developed a method that used a deep level of mind power to create a heightened awareness that surpassed all original intentions. He found that the mind could obtain information directly through the spiritual dimension that taps into coincidence, intuition, and psychic ability.

Even more interesting is the underlying principle that plays a pivotal role in Jose Silva's Ultramind ESP System. To qualify for this help from higher intelligence, you must be involved in constructive and creative activities that make this a better world in which to live. In Jose Silva's words, we are not rewarded for what we take, but for what we give. When you lift up humanity, you are also lifting up yourself because you are a part of humanity. When you help other people, especially people who are hurting, you will have many successes.

"We cannot hold a torch to light another person's path without brightening our own."—Ben Sweetland, author of *Grow Rich While You Sleep*

You have been introduced to many different models, theories, and systems that aim for very similar goals and outcomes. When you seek to bring out the best in yourself and others; the results are profoundly rewarding. True, this can be a tall order. It is easy to forget the magic and delicacy of life. People come and go in the blink of an eye. In hindsight, how often do you consider why you made such a big deal out of something? How often do you wish you would have done or said things differently? Well, it is never too late. Today is a new day that can mark the beginning of a new you with a fresh outlook and renewed relationships. Decide to be *the one* to rise above pettiness that undermines relationships and lead yourself and others towards all the benefits of connecting in a much deeper and more harmonious way.

"The Ultimate lesson all of us have to learn is unconditional love, which includes not only others but ourselves as well."—Elisabeth Kubler-Ross, M.D., psychiatrist and author of *On Death and Dying*.

Keys to Effective Communication in Business And Personal Relationships
Written By Rita Simon Fata

"Wait a minute—I'm talking!" "Let me finish!" "Stop interrupting!" "Shhhhhhhh!!" "You didn't hear a word I said!" Sound familiar? Of course it does. We interrupt each other all the time. Everyone seems to have a lot to say and wants to be heard. So, very often, we all speak at the same time. Is it any wonder, then, that we frequently walk away from a conversation without any idea of what was said?

Are your business and personal relationships not working as well as you'd like? Maybe you are having difficulty because you are not really listening to what the other person, the speaker, is saying. Failing to understand the true meaning of what is being said is not inconsequential. Thinking, almost entirely, about what we want to say and not fully appreciating and incorporating the speaker's information and perspective into our own thought processes, is bound to result in imperfect and incomplete insight into any given topic.

When we fail to listen effectively, we deprive ourselves of the benefit of understanding ideas and opinions that the speaker is communicating. Often, we describe those who remain unaware as being "out of touch" or "clueless." However, the flipside of faulty hearing is knowledge, which is gained when we are cognizant of the written word and the spoken word. If we are oblivious to the meanings of words or incapable of knowing how to hear them, we will never be fully informed or enlightened. Thus, we will forfeit our ability to comprehend what is relevant and important.

Hearing is not the same as listening. We may hear every sound that is spoken but not grasp what was said. Listening is an important skill that is a key component of communication. Listening is an expression of true caring and forms our foundation for capturing the essence of the spoken word. Without the ability to listen, our threshold of comprehension is severely limited, and our hope of communicating completely is diminished. That is why it is important that we take the time to give full attention to the speaker. We must not waste our time over-emphasizing lyrical messages, catchy phrases, or bullet points. Instead, we must learn to discover the true meaning of actual words that are spoken and the message that they are conveying so that we can come to appreciate the value of exact interpretation. Once we are able to do so, we will find that our ability to communicate effectively will increase tenfold.

As children, we are all taught basic communication skills. We start by learning to talk, then read, and, finally, write. But there is no formal training or even mention of a skill that we spend half our time doing—that is, listening. Instead, the emphasis is placed on learning to talk. But, if only we were taught how to listen, we would be in a much better position to learn the skill that is fundamental to our ability to communicate with each other in a meaningful and effective way. How can we be expected to answer a question completely; take accurate notes; or sustain awareness if we fail to grasp the detail of what is being said?

So, let's take some time to acknowledge the value of centering our focus on developing one of our most practical and productive senses. We will not take any shortcuts by defining important points casually or capriciously. Instead, we will concentrate on the importance of being able to hear the spoken word, recognizing the implicit and explicit meanings attached to each sentence or phrase, and the significance of mannerisms and style employed by the speaker.

No doubt, we all have memories of being in a classroom and raising our hands before the teacher finished talking. Most of us can probably recall attending a seminar and trying to make a point before the end of a speech. How many times have we found ourselves at a meeting focusing on what we will say before the meeting has ended? Not only are we behaving badly by interrupting the person who is speaking, we are also violating the speaker's right to be heard. Through our own actions, we ultimately deprive ourselves of the opportunity to fully understand what is being said, which is the cornerstone of having complete and satisfying knowledge.

Thus, it follows that remaining silent can be one of our most productive skills. When we are quiet while someone is speaking, our silence tells the speaker that:

1. I want to take the time to hear what you are saying.

2. I want you to continue speaking, as I am interested in what you are saying.

3. I respect your right to be heard.

Although we may be able to hear perfectly and are committed to taking the time to listen, it does not necessarily mean that we will fully appreciate what was actually said. It is easy and, unfortunately, commonplace to miss the main point(s). Can you remember being in any of the following situations?

1. As soon as introductions are made, you forget the name(s) of the individual(s) being presented.

2. When you first hear a story and then repeat it to someone else, do you ever find that you don't recall a particular detail and say, "Pardon me, but I can't seem to remember…," or "Now, what was the point I was trying to make?"

3. What about when a story is told, over and over, until the final version has almost nothing in common with the original? While we all may find humor in failing to accurately describe what was said, an underlying and important point is that we all possess a different span of attention and erratic memory that can impart different meaning to identical words and phrases.

4. Do you ever forget just about everything that was told to you shortly after it was said?

No doubt, we all probably answered yes to one or more of the previous questions so it is possible to conclude that we don't always hear what was said. It is likely that we were listening but, because our listening skills are inadequate, we often miss part or all of what is being communicated. All too often, we become passive about listening. We tend to combine listening with thinking about things other than what a speaker is saying. We do not allot adequate time to listening. That being said, let's take note of exactly what listening is and what it is not.

First and foremost, listening is:

1. Turning your full attention to the person who is speaking.

2. Focusing not only on the verbal, but also the visual.

3. Disciplined and time consuming.

4. Hearing what is being said and gaining new insight from it.

Listening is not:

1. Instinctive or mechanical.

2. Waiting for your turn to talk.

3. Mindless imitation of the speaker's words.

4. Fast or quick.

In the world of business, listening is a powerful tool. Being a good listener enables us to understand those with whom we associate. When we listen effectively, it is likely that we will become more keenly aware of potential problems and be in a better position to develop solutions. No doubt, the need for owners of businesses and managers to fully understand what was said is critical to the decision making process.

To its credit, technology has played an important role in streamlining many processes. To its detriment, personal interaction has decreased as a result of some of these changes, and sometimes nothing can replace the value of communication that is gained through discussions that take place in face-to-face meetings. Personal contact remains essential to forming trusted and lasting business relationships. Frequently, a client will avoid disclosing confidential information in e-mail, no matter how secure a system may be. The trust that develops through personal contact is priceless in any business environment. When a client shares important or confidential information with us, it is vital that we fully understand the client's position and respond appropriately. We must always exhibit patience and take as much time as needed to connect with our client on all levels.

At home, there is probably no other skill as meaningful or productive as listening. Understanding a spouse or partner is vital to maintaining open, healthy, and happy relationships. Children often find it difficult to express their feelings. Therefore, as parents, we must take the time to not only answer questions, but pose them as well. We will gain greater understanding if we go out of our way to take the initiative to be thoughtful and considerate.

Now that we have defined what "listening" is and is not, it is important to understand that there are other components of communication that often convey messages that words do not. For example, "body language" can speak volumes. Let's take a look at some of the following gestures and what meaning they could impart:

1. A speaker whose arms are folded or placed on the hips can convey a negative message of stiffness or control; while a speaker whose posture is relaxed comes across as open and free.

2. Failure to make eye contact can imply insecurity and diminish credibility. A speaker who engages the audience, by looking at everyone, expresses interest and trust.

3. Foot tapping or jerky hand motions can be interpreted as signs of nervousness and be distracting.

Finally, it is also important to understand the significance of what is unspoken. Sometimes a statement that something will be done might truly mean that something will not be done. Conversely, a statement that something will not be done may convey that something will be done. We must keep this in mind when we analyze a speaker's statements so that we not only gain complete knowledge of the subject and are also fully aware of what actions will or will not be taken. Eliminating certain words can be deliberate and have more impact than any words that are included. Therefore, we should not be surprised if unspoken words are more compelling than their counterparts. For example, a salesman tells you everything that is right with the product he wants you to buy. But what is the salesman not saying? Exclusions can be very telling.

Let us remember that we must also be able to acknowledge that true meaning may be elusive because our perceptions are often colored by emotion, past experiences, or the physical environment. During the course of listening, we must be able to identify and silence haunting triggers so that we do not fall prey to responding to emotion by ignoring dialogue. Listening demands that we be quiet, calm, patient, and informed.

How we respond to a speaker demonstrates the effectiveness of our listening skills. An owner or manager of a business cannot communicate effectively or productively with colleagues, vendors, or staff without understanding what is really being said. Likewise, husbands and wives will not be in a position to reach out to each other or their children in an open or meaningful way if they fail to devote their full attention to what is being said. Therefore, after listening to any speaker, our responses should be:

1. Accepting so that the speaker understands that the topic was meaningful.

2. Interesting so that the speaker concludes that the message was received.

3. Respectful so that the speaker is comfortable answering candidly and open to revealing more.

Listening provides opportunities to build better relationships and enables us to become more adept at resolving conflicts. In school, good listening skills can determine whether a student passes or fails. In the office, there will be fewer mistakes if the employee has taken the time to listen and absorb what was said. At home, we can form more respectful and trusting relationships and avoid arguments by taking the time to hear what we are all saying.

Now that we have learned how to listen and what to listen for, we must take the time to find occasions to listen so that communication can flourish. Whether in your office or at home, consider creating some of the following opportunities for exchange:

1. Schedule regular times to talk.

2. Maintain an "open door" policy.

3. Engage others in conversation; don't wait for someone to talk to you first.

4. Discover mutual areas of interest and explore them.

5. Relate important ideas as a means of soliciting feedback.

6. Be trustful and also trustworthy.

Once we have perfected our listening skills, it follows that verbal exchanges will become more meaningful and productive. We will find it easier to maintain a direct focus so that central themes will become more readily apparent. Instinctively, we will know what to listen for. Eventually, we may even spend more time listening than speaking.

Providing the speaker with feedback is an important element in communication. However, we must remember to make it a point to never interrupt the speaker or ask questions that are distracting or divert attention away from the speaker's topic. Let's be open, receptive, and responsive. Let's communicate with the speaker with feeling and enthusiasm. Let's be prepared to listen by managing our thought processes so that we are able to stay anchored in the moment of the spoken word.

Over time, listening can develop into an integral part of our communication skills. As an accomplished listener, we will find it much easier to command attention when we have something to say. How should we engage our audience—whether it be one person or many? What skills should we employ? Here are some to consider:

1. Develop a style that makes the listener feel relaxed and comfortable. Know something about the person or audience you are speaking to. For example, is the listener (or your audience) someone who is very serious? Enjoys humor? Needs a lot of explanation? Comfortable with jargon? Structure your delivery accordingly.

2. Be open so that you don't distance yourself from the listener. Welcome frank comments and feedback even if your point of view is being challenged.

3. Be revealing. Share something personal about yourself that you think will make you interesting and approachable.

4. Do not fail to notice how the listener is responding to you. Are you achieving the results that you anticipated? Be prepared to make some changes if you are not.

5. Don't hesitate to inject humor into your speech; but be careful so that you do not offend. A humorous aside about yourself is appropriate. Making an example of the listener or someone in your audience usually is not.

6. Speak clearly; be relevant, and substantive. Know your topic thoroughly and answer all questions that are posed in a credible and detailed manner.

7. Make sure the listener feels good about you and looks forward to speaking with you again. Be caring, thoughtful, and sincere when responding.

The capacity for in-depth understanding is a powerful tool. Our ability to listen and convey meaning forms a basis for mutual exchange that can be the starting point for building timeless and meaningful personal and professional relationships. Listen carefully, and you will clearly hear what is being said. Be expressive and appropriate when responding so that your words convey wisdom and relevance. Above all, be generous with your time as well as your spirit so that your accomplishment is genuinely rewarding.

Seven Steps For Finding The Love of Your Life
Written By Laura Kobus

Imagine being in a relationship with someone you love being with and who brings out the best in you. You are extremely compatible and feel completely at ease with them. Although this person knows your weaknesses, they are still supportive and nurturing. The relationship is easy and harmonious with a comfortable balance of give and take. And as an extra bonus—they make you laugh. If this sounds impossible, think again. Here are seven steps you can take to find the love you've always dreamed of.

1.   **Develop a Strong Sense of Self.** Strengthen your identity and get in touch with the real you by embarking on a journey of self-discovery. This may include the development of new or existing hobbies, a spiritual practice, journaling or dates with yourself where you can spend time alone doing what you love or simply in quiet contemplation. You will be amazed at the increased awareness and confidence this process brings. When you look to others to give you a sense of identity, or to complete you, you surrender your power to them. It's like setting yourself up for a high speed roller coaster ride, because when everything is going well, you are coasting smoothly, but if they become disapproving or decide they want out of the relationship, you come crashing to the ground. This is a very stressful way to live.

     Contemplative Questions:

     Who am I?

     What are my strongest values?

2. **Evaluate Your Belief System.** When your beliefs are in alignment with your goals, you are much more likely to hit your target. If you've reached the stage where you exclaim "There are no good men/women left," you will probably find that to be true. Another possibility is that even though you tell yourself that you're willing and ready to meet that special someone, deep down you may not feel you really deserve to.

Contemplative Questions:

What beliefs do I have about myself or the opposite sex that may be holding me back from meeting my ideal mate?

What new beliefs am I willing to substitute?

3. **Get Clear on What You Want in a Mate.** Just as an architect starts with a blueprint before building a home, everyone should have a blueprint for their ideal relationship. Since some of us know what we don't want more than what we do want, the first step is to use the table provided to make a list of ten to fifteen qualities you *don't* want in a partner. Next, list the opposite in the second column. You probably will not have fifteen qualities immediately nor should you expect to. In time you may think of more, in which case you can add them to your list later.

What I *Don't* Want	The Opposite (What I *Do* Want)
1.	
2.	
3.	
4.	
5.	
6.	
7.	
8.	
9.	
10.	
11.	
12.	
13.	
14.	
15.	

Congratulations! You've just created the profile of your ideal partner in column two.

Next, highlight or circle the qualities that you absolutely *must have* in someone. Do the same for the *deal breakers* (qualities that are unacceptable and would end a relationship) in column one. The qualities left that are not highlighted or circled are ones that can be compromised.

Now scan the profile of your ideal partner again and put an asterisk next to those qualities that aren't totally true about you.

Contemplative Question:

How can I develop those qualities more in myself?

Now wait a minute, why must I have those qualities?" you might ask. "Don't opposites attract?" Yes they can, but remember that the concept "like attracts like" is even more powerful. The more you have in common with someone, the greater the odds of the relationship succeeding.

Doing the exercise is quite powerful. If you use your profile as a guideline when you meet someone new, it will help to rule out people who are not right for you and hone in on those who are. This gets you as close as possible to finding your ideal mate. What you put out to the universe is what you will attract, so be sure that what you wish for is exactly what you want.

4. **Practice the Law of Attraction.** Your thoughts create your reality. I've found that when I'm in a social situation and feeling worried or negative, I attract people who are quite eager to bombard me with their complaints about themselves and the world. However, when I'm smiling, feeling happy and carefree, people and situations I attract are of a positive nature. Have you ever awakened one morning and said to yourself, "I'm not feeling so great; this is going to be a rotten day" and then watched Murphy's Law in action as one bad thing after another happened? Maybe your car wouldn't start, then someone cut you off on the road, then you got into an argument with a co-worker, etc.

    Another more tangible example of how "like attracts like" is to observe a tuning fork. If you ding a tuning fork in a room filled with all different kinds of tuning forks calibrated to various pitches, only the ones calibrated to the *same frequency* as the one you just dinged will ding too.

    Start experimenting with the Law of Attraction on a regular basis. The next time you are on a date or at a social gathering, even if you're not feeling good, act as if you are and you will ultimately feel better. Your brain doesn't know the difference. Focus on the abundance in your life rather than the lack. Smile, stand tall, speak with confidence and send good vibrations out to others. In essence, put your attention only on the results you want to see. Then watch what kind of response you get. When you realize the power your thoughts can have, you may want to be very careful of what you think about!

Contemplative Question:

How can I shift my attitude or behavior to ensure that I attract only people and circumstances that are for my highest good?

5. **Have a Satisfying Life.** When you are happy in your job or career and surround yourself with people and activities that you find fun and exciting, your life is rich and full. Therefore, when you enter into a relationship without feeling needy, you are in a position to give and truly enjoy the other person. Have you ever dated someone who relied on you for their sole source of pleasure and entertainment? If so, your first instinct was probably to get out from under that pressure as quickly as possible.

Contemplative Question:

How can I make my life richer while seeking my ideal partner?

6. **Take Action.** The only way your ideal mate will come knocking on your door is if s/he is a traveling salesperson. Remember the commercial for Lotto, "You've got to be in it to win it?" Well, the same holds true for dating—you've got to be in the game to score a mate. There are many ways to meet someone but the important thing is that you participate in activities you enjoy where you'll find members of the opposite sex. Start with your own interests. If you like the arts, visit a museum or attend a gallery opening. If music and dancing are your passion, go to a concert, night club or take singles dance lessons. Internet dating has become very popular and can be quite successful as long as you are discerning. The important thing is to just get going.

Here are twenty-one ways to meet the love of your life.

1) Online Dating
2) Singles Groups
3) Work
4) Bookstores
5) Libraries
6) House of Worship
7) Coffee Shops
8) Athletic Clubs
9) School
10) Sporting Events
11) Museums
12) Parks and Beaches
13) Art Galleries
14) Parties
15) Introductions
16) Dating Services
17) Concerts
18) Nightclubs
19) Volunteer or Fund Raising Organizations
20) Waiting Rooms
21) Classes and Conferences

Contemplative Question:

Which of these options do I want to try first?

7. **Determine Your Compatibility.** Listed are thirteen areas of compatibility. List your criteria for the categories directly below each one. Feel free to add any categories that are not mentioned.

Example: What is your criteria for ambition? If you want your partner to be a high achiever, then write "high achiever" under ambition. If your criteria for appearance is someone at least 5'8" tall, slim, attractive, and neat, indicate that under appearance.

Ambition   Financial

Appearance   Personality

Character   Religion/Spirituality

Communication   Sense of Humor

Education   Sexuality

Emotional Makeup   Values

Family   _____

_____   _____

When you have your criteria for each category, ask yourself the following question. *"Does my potential partner meet these criteria?"* Since most people will not meet all, consider which are most important to you in a relationship.

When meeting someone new, listed are nine questions to ask yourself in order to identify if you're on the right track for romance.

1) Is this person reasonably healthy (physically and emotionally) and available for a relationship?
2) Am I attracted to them?
3) Do they seem sincere?
4) Do I enjoy being in their presence?
5) Do they treat me with kindness and respect?
6) Do we have similar values and goals?
7) Do they have a sense of humor?
8) Do we communicate effectively with each other?
9) Do they bring out the best in me?

Contemplative Question:

Now that I know who's right for me, am I ready to go for it?

Connections with other human beings, particularly our most intimate relationships, are the true substance of life. In the end, they are what really matter most. Now that you are more in tune with yourself and what you want, jump into the dating pool and start swimming. That great catch is out there and just might be swimming toward you right now.

Chapter Four:
Finding A Career With Meaning And Purpose

What Career Will Bring You Meaning And Purpose?
Written By Leslie Malin

How do we choose a career that will provide us with a sense of "rightness," of being 'on purpose' and capable of shaping us in meaningful ways? In my 25 years as a therapist, coach, workshop facilitator and career consultant I have seen that question enliven and embolden people as well as cripple and stall them. To grasp the enormity of this question we must break it down into small and manageable parts, otherwise it is so big and fraught with worry, uncertainty and self-doubt that people abandon the search before they start the journey.

My own experience has been diverse. And that's not including creating a costume jewelry business and co-creating a greeting card company! And often these endeavors were done simultaneously. Perhaps from the outside looking in, this sounds fractured. However, each endeavor that I have engaged in has more fully defined who I am, what I love, what I thrive on as well as the flip sides of these—who I am not, what I can't abide, what deflates and de-values me. And, all along the way my understanding of meaning and purpose has expanded, coalesced, and redesigned itself.

What I realize from this vantage point is that everything I have been drawn to has been woven with the same basic threads even if the design has appeared radically different at certain times. The common threads have been: assisting others in finding their way, expressing myself creatively, communicating effectively and, above all else, growing, learning, exploring and taking chances. It is only now that I have fully comprehended that my career always had meaning and purpose even if at times I was challenged by it, overwhelmed with it, and had fits of anxiety and panic about it.

And, everything you have done in your life is embedded with meaning and purpose because your life has meaning and purpose whether you realize it or not. Even our failures, missteps and lost opportunities are the ingredients of creating and defining what will have value as we go forward. As the saying goes, "The only people who have never made a mistake are people who have never done anything." So often, I have worked with talented, caring and earnest people who feel immobilized when they seek to uncover their Meaning and Purpose to *bless their work*. These concepts have become so elevated and almost saintly that I fear they have become the newest "ism" to make people feel inadequate and insufficient.

We Grant Ourselves Meaning And Purpose

Meaning and purpose come from how you engage in your work and life. No career regardless of how lofty, giving or self-sacrificing grants meaning. We alone are grantors of our life's meaning and purpose. We alone find it worthy or not, on purpose or not.

Once you begin to equate meaning and purpose with specific kinds of outcomes you will fail to embrace the meaning and purpose that continues to exist even when the outcomes become messier than you believe possible. Many of my clients and friends have gone along in successful careers and suddenly the bottom falls out and they feel like failures or fools. They are neither, they are just being called to re-examine where they are at this particular point in their lives and discover what is calling them forward. Others have remained in jobs or businesses that have long been drained of meaning, but were too fearful or unready to move out into uncharted territory. Sometimes, those careers and jobs can be resurrected if you become involved in them in new and creative ways; and sometimes one needs to move out and become an adventurer. And, in our era many have become slaves of high tech and new management styles and become what Simon Head, author of "The New Ruthless Economy," calls "digital assembly lines" that appear to offer little opportunity for imagination, creativity or even relationship building. Thus, they are stripped of meaning being designed as automation functions rather than human endeavors.

Meaning and purpose are large and dynamic questions that can only be learned through experience not through some careful, linear approach. And while we seem to be more frequently searching for these sustaining underpinnings to our work, they are becoming more and more elusive. In part, I think this is because we believe that <u>Our</u> Meaning and Purpose have to be hugely significant to qualify as deserving of such a title. Therefore, we may tend to overlook our real value because we think it too mundane or small. Like so much else in our complex lives and often competitive lives, meaning and purpose have become badges of honor and self-promotion. Thus, really locating what's truly meaningful to us can become another exercise in "Am I good enough? Is my purpose sufficiently big? And is my meaning as good as his/her meaning?" rather than being an authentic discovery of what we feel is our unique calling. As Caroline Myss has noted, sometimes our purpose is only to be the "light" in some remote corner of Wyoming, not some major celebrity on Oprah.

To complicate this even further, how we define these elements can be as unique as each of us. What I believe will invest my career and life with purpose and meaning will probably look very different than yours. The big lesson here is, don't compare yourself to others; your road to meaning is yours and yours alone.

As a young person straight out of college we may choose to pursue a profession or specific industry, but often the issues of meaning and purpose are immediate, reality bound and survival focused: What will bring me enough money? What will give me the status or jumping off point I desire? What will offer the experience and learning I need to advance? How will others judge this?

Some who feel limited by lack of education, resources or other challenges choose jobs that others consider meaningless and yet they discover wondrous ways to inhabit those jobs/careers with enormous meaning. In a recent editorial in the *New York Times*, Adam Cohen wrote about how difficult it is to find meaning in today's workplace compared to three decades ago. Thirty years ago Cohen says, Studs Terkel wrote about the thoughts of ordinary Americans who were rarely heard from—bellhops, waitresses, even gravediggers. And he discovered that, "even for the lowliest laborers, work was a search, sometimes successful, sometimes not, 'for daily meaning as well as daily bread.'"

Others head early into a life of "meaning" and have regrets later in their lives regarding what they may have sacrificed or disregarded when they made those choices. Our lives and the meaning of our lives and work often only become manifest once we have garnered experience, accumulated some scuffs and bruises along the way and developed some wisdom about ourselves and our world.

Please, don't misunderstand me. I am not saying that asking this question is meaningless or must be put off for another time. What I am suggesting is that the place to begin is to turn the question around and rather than ask the "What" questions right away we can begin by asking ourselves the "Who" questions.

Try To Love The Questions Themselves…

I encourage you to take sufficient time to ask yourselves these following questions and to thoughtfully answer them *in writing*. Writing down our thoughts and feelings signals the universe that we are serious about discovering the answers. It indicates to our deeper being that we are honoring ourselves and valuing our lives. Writing them down becomes a record of who we were in a particular moment in time and allows us to chart our progress over time. I have found it an exciting realization that even when I have felt that I hadn't made any movement (when looking for the *outward* manifestation) that I had most often accomplished significant *inside* shifts that were required as preparation prior to the budding of movement or accomplishment.

Be patient toward all that is unsolved in your heart and try to love the questions themselves…Do not now seek the answers which cannot be given you because you would not be able to live them and the point is to live everything. Live the questions now. Perhaps you will then gradually, without noticing it, live along some distant day into the answer.—Rainer Maria Rilke

Let these questions linger inside you for a while, live them; journal your responses; share them with trusted friends and advisors, and see what natural course of action presents itself as a result.

- Who am I at this particular moment?
- What do I respect about myself—the little often nameless acts and ways of being that really define me to me?
- What value or special-ness do others think I offer? How am I seen though eyes other than my own?
- What have I yet to learn? What kinds of experiences could yield that knowledge?
- What or who do I love and cherish, right now? Why?
- What challenges excite me and invites me to grow?
- What frightens me?
- Where is my self-doubt greater than my self-love?
- Where do I lose my power?
- What empowers me?

- Where do I stand up for what I believe? Where do I stand back?
- Where am I in my life path—just starting out, in the middle, or even further along? What has been meaningful to me to this point?
- What have I experienced at work to this point (that could mean parenting, volunteer work, internships, anything) that has felt fulfilling, challenging, and growth-filled? What aspects created those experiences? What aspects were draining, dispiriting or just plain dull?
- Where does career place in the context of other demands, expectations and desires that exist for me at this time?
- What makes this question of creating meaning and purpose in my career so important?
- What am I afraid will happen if I can't figure out what career will bring meaning and purpose?

These questions and others like them, bring us back to ourselves. Questions and answers are just forms of energy—they are neither good nor bad; or smart nor dumb unless we define them as so, unless we tell ourselves a story about what are the "good" things to think and the "bad" things to think. However, if you take these questions as a form of meditation, where meaning is allowed to surface as and when it decides you can discover much meaning and truth.

Once you begin to tackle these questions, you will discover much about what gives you joy, excitement, enthusiasm, courage and self-respect. It is these outcomes that shape meaning and purpose. Let's say I was a hospice worker, meaningful and valuable work to be sure. However, if I didn't derive a sense of well-being from it, if I didn't learn something valuable about my life and life in general, if I left feeling devastated and overcome each day then, for me, the job would feel meaningless and purposeless. How many people have entered careers that they believed would grant them meaning and purpose and how many have left these jobs feeling like something was wrong with them and that they were failures?

A Career Emerges From the Inside Out

A career has meaning and purpose when you experience that it does. It's something that comes from the inside out.

Some of you may be feeling impatient and perhaps a bit anxious at this point. "I need a guide, not some suggestions about asking myself countless questions, the answers to which seem obscure if not downright irrelevant. Can't you just give me a formula, provide a step-by-step outline and get me there quickly and painlessly? This is going to take just too much time! I've got to get going, I'm already 25, 35, 55, etc."

Of course, there are linear, step-by-step approaches, but in my experience they are premature if not preceded by the inner journey. Crafting a life and work of meaning is a hard job. It demands much of us because it can provide so much in return. What is easily won is rarely long-lived or valued. What we fight and struggle for is most often what we value, what grants us self-esteem and what shapes us. And yet, we back away from the interior approach because of fear. Fear of disorder, fear of confusion, fear of just hanging out in the unknown. If we continue to feed our fear by sidestepping the unknown we grow monsters that lurk in every corner.

Look to the lives of many people whom we consider to be giant role models and you will often find a similar refrain—sounding very much like anguish and despair—they didn't fit in, they were out of step with their times, they felt they had lost their way, that they were alone and they screamed "What more do you want of me anyway?"

And, the answer to that question is often, "You must listen. You must go quiet inside. You must embrace uncertainty and disorder"; and, to do all these things while still doing the grocery shopping, going to work, dealing with our friends and families and taking care of the mundane things of our existence. Then, often unannounced, something cracks open; the time comes when the pain of staying contained is more than the pain of emerging.

Appointment with Destiny

On a beautiful day in 1995, I was walking down Fifth Avenue in New York City having just left an appointment with a client. I strolled past Barnes & Noble and there, sitting in the window was a display of a simply designed paperback book, *Creating the Work You Love: Courage, Commitment and Career* by Rick Jarow. Immediately and powerfully drawn into the store I bought this book which was to have a vast impact on my thinking, my life and my work. Here is the last paragraph of the second chapter of this book, followed by my comments in the margin.

"If we really asked why, or better yet, if we really observed how we live—seeing the hurry and the haste, the devaluation of entire classes of people, the lack of connectedness with the very world that surrounds us—we would have to face the terrible void that we try to cover with business, productivity, and politics. If we want to integrate our work we have to challenge the status-quo consensus—we have to take the responsibility to become truly healthy. To be healthy is to be right with the world—its people, creatures and rhythms. No one else will make it right for us, for our essential nature is unique to each of us. To return to essence is to return to inner balance and such balance is the only basis from which a true career can be created (italics are mine)."

My scribbled notes: *"Can't believe this! This is what I've been saying—trying to move towards. WOW-talk about responding to my intuition...Barnes and Noble window calling out to me!"*

I was thrilled that I wasn't alone; Jarow was asking and answering the same questions and through a number of years of studying with him I met many pilgrims like myself along the way.

Jarow writes of crafting an "anti-career, a throwing off of the shackles of obligation, approval and mindless activity in order to enter deeply into the dynamics of co-creation. To make your work sacred is to believe in what you do. To do a good job is its own reward, and is to feel proud of your work not by comparing it to the work of others but by feeling good inside, filled with integrity, neither fatigued nor drained of energy."

These Dreams Are Made For Walking

OK, so now we are listening and dreaming and beginning to understand, but that is not enough. We need to bring those refrains we hear, those dreams we spin and those understandings that are unfolding into the world. We must find the courage to begin to manifest them and let them be tested—we must find a way to let them live.

And, like bringing anything into life—birthing is fraught with fear, anxiety and uncertainty. How will my fragile beginnings be received in the world? Will they be found not beautiful or sufficiently worthy? Will they be ridiculed...Will I? Once the process of birth begins, so does the reality of separation and loss of control. Will you be able to stand your ground when all around you others may be saying that you are being foolish, wasting time, being unrealistic or terribly naïve?

For more years than I care to count, I was surrounded by people who accused me of wasting my talents, going off into too many directions, not having a viable business plan, being imprudent and even reckless. Some would chuckle amongst themselves, "Oh, there is Leslie again, what is she doing now!" or would provide condescending and paternalistic advice which, they believed, I was being obstinate not to adopt. I don't really know how I didn't buckle and succumb, sometimes I agreed with their assessment, but I couldn't back away from the fire of my knowing. Deep inside me, however, I knew I had to find a way to weave all these skeins together because to abandon one was to abandon myself.

I'm sharing this because I want to share with you that it takes courage, patience and fortitude to set off looking for meaning and purpose. Like Dorothy in the Wizard of OZ, we can be snatched up in a terrifying tornado and land in an unknown parallel universe which is both alien and yet quite familiar. Like Dorothy we need to find faith, allies, courage, compassion, authenticity and loyalty while continuing to walk along our yellow brick road. Dorothy could only find the way home when she comes home to herself. And coming home to ourselves is, as Jarow has observed, inextricably linked to "genuine self acceptance, (which) translates into self-respect, which becomes self-reliance."

There are many roads we can take to "come home," and one of the scariest yet most fruitful is to begin to have what I call, *Courageous Conversations*. I've suggested that first you ask yourself questions and more questions and more questions, but there comes a time when we need to take the dialogue out into the world—another birthing.

Courageous Conversations

The first theme might be "I intend to…" Begin with imaginary conversations. What do you really want to tell people about yourself? What is begging to be let free?

1. Who are the people that are most important or terrifying to you that you know you must declare yourself to? List them and then prioritize them.

2. Practice these imaginary conversations with all the detail you can image—where you would be, what time of day, what would you be wearing, what would they? How would they respond, how might they respond in ways you don't expect?

3. Start by saying the words out loud. Don't stop when you choke up or sputter or get lost. Just start again from the beginning.

4. Notice what you are experiencing: Is it fear, anxiety, panic, anger, shame, resentment or something else?

Don't analyze yourself or try to talk yourself out what you are experiencing, just embrace the feelings, thank them for trying to protect you from harm, and tell them you are strong enough to go on. Keep doing this for a day, a week or a month, whatever it takes until you feel solid and clear.

Taking The Conversation On The Road:

OK, now we are done with dress rehearsals and ready for the actual performance.

1. Thoughtfully choose the time and place. Make an appointment with yourself for a specific conversation. People sometimes want to impulsively jump into these conversations, but I believe that they are sacred. They are your first brave announcements of new beginnings and they deserve planning, time and perhaps even some ritual before beginning.
2. If it helps, start with the most receptive person first.
3. Breathe. You can't believe how many people stop breathing and then choke up.
4. Take your time. Try not to rush it.
5. Ask that they listen first without giving you any feedback—perhaps at this stage, you really don't want any feedback at all—neither negative or positive. You just want to say out loud what has been raging inside for so long.

6. Debrief what happened when you are alone. Or share the preparation, rehearsal, and performance with a trusted friend, coach, therapist, or other.

    a. First of all congratulate yourself for your courage and fortitude.

    b. List everything you liked about what you said and how you said it.

    c. What could be improved in the next conversation?

    d. What did you discover?

    e. What surprised you?

    f. What embarrassed, saddened, frightened or threw you?

    g. What were your greatest lessons?

    h. What new tools do you have for the next Courageous Conversation?

As these conversations move from the imaginary to the real, they take on weight, substance and form. They are commitments—not necessarily to a specific form of action or time line—but a commitment to moving forward. They are a commitment to walking the road, not knowing necessarily where it will take you, but trusting that the road is the essential ground beneath your feet and it is from walking this ground that you discover "home."

In the Bible it says, that "in the beginning was the Word and the Word was good." Every tradition tells that the beginning of creation began with "the Word," out of the vastness of unconsciousness comes material reality in the form of sound and words. And, that is how we can evolve our reality as well. Our words create a kind of a force field, words are powerful and they can propel us forward or turn against us depending upon what we say.

Now that we have articulated and communicated our intentions, it's time to begin to take small, daily steps towards actualizing our dream. Those steps can be taking a class, writing an outline, painting, meeting with new people, doing research, it doesn't actually matter. What matters is that you stay in action. When we take action, regardless of how small, we are in communion with our deepest selves, when we are in such a relationship with ourselves our actions feel effortless, we'll say, "wow, I was in the zone."

Assemble A Team

There is nothing more powerful than to reach out and put together a team of competent, knowledgeable and committed people who believe in you and what you want to have in your life and work. Sometimes we are surrounded by them and all we need to do reach out and ask and at other times, we need to search for new people who have a different view of what is possible and will enthusiastically support us in our quest.

On teams there are different functions and amounts of involvement. Perhaps you could benefit from a professional team that could include teachers, therapists, coaches, and people with specific expertise (web designers, writers, marketing people, and the like). Others could be colleagues or friends who are positive, self-actualizing, energetic, pragmatic, practical, detail oriented, or who have other traits that can support or complement your strengths and weaknesses and are willing to be there for you. You can create strategic alliances where you create "contracts" with others for mutual benefit. The point is, we don't achieve anything alone. We live in relationship and that is an enormous source of strength.

As you move out of the realm of the envisioning you begin to walk the path of the Hero. In a wonderful book called, *Zen and the Art of Making a Living: A Practical Guide to Creative Career Design* by Laurence G. Boldt the Hero is described as follows:

> "...the Hero is the inner King or Queen, the chooser, the decider, the one who gives direction, who sets the life course... The Hero bravely enters into the dark forest of the unknown, and once, through great effort, he sees the light, he is determined to live by the light that he sees. Because his vision, or clarity, is hard won, he is not easily dissuaded from his insights.
>
> ...The Hero exercises the judgment that selects out what is worthy of his or her time, attention and energy, that is worthy of his or her life. To choose a life direction is the Hero's greatest choice."

You are on a great adventure; you are singular but not alone. Your companions are inspiration, imagination, perception, intuition, faith, courage, determination, knowledge, friendship and community. Focus on your Being and meaningful Doing will follow.

Discover Your Ideal Career
Written By Laura Kobus

Do you spend your workdays dragging yourself through the day, wishing it would end so you could move on to your "real life?" Now imagine the opposite scenario. You are so energized and passionate about your work that you lose all track of time!

So what's stopping you from finding work you love? For many it's the belief that they can't make a living at what they really like doing. Others don't even have the slightest inkling as to what they would like to do.

The good news is that you *can* find work you love *and* make a decent living at it. How do I know this? Because I spent many years in jobs I disliked, wishing for more fulfilling work, but having no idea as to what it was. Finally, the day came when I simply had to make a change. Through a process which I will share with you, I realized that I wanted a career helping others overcome the same challenges that I had undergone. I discovered that working as a personal and career coach would be a great fit for me. After completing my training and starting a practice, I realized my decision proved correct. Now I can say that I love what I do and am making a living at it too. Here are four steps for finding your ideal career.

Step 1: Begin Your Journey By Looking Within. If you're wondering where you should start, the answer is "with yourself." The self-inventory process that follows will provide you with the clarity you need to take your next steps.

Contemplative Questions:

Write the answer that comes to mind for each question or statement.

> *List five things you loved to do as a child.*

> *List five things that would truly excite you if they were on your calendar tomorrow.*

Recall a time when you were so completely alive and happy that you thought, "This is what life is all about!" What were you doing? Describe the feelings and values being expressed.

What would you do if you knew you couldn't fail?

What job would you perform even if you didn't receive any pay?

If you had one year left to live and money was no object, how would you spend that year?

Reviewing your work history, when and where did you find the greatest satisfaction, interest or fulfillment?

List five or more activities, functions or responsibilities you would like in a position.

List five or more activities, functions or responsibilities you would not like as significant parts of your next position.

List five fantasy jobs you would consider if money, education and experience were no barrier. Really go wild here! List this job even if it doesn't exist.

Do you have any family commitments or other restrictions that would influence what type of job you would choose? (Example: People with children or aging/ill family members may want a flexible working schedule).

Strengths, Skills, Interests, Values:

List your top **FIVE** for each category. Note: If you have trouble identifying them, think of what others (including your friends, family, boss and colleagues) would say about you. You may even want to ask them.

STRENGTHS/POSITIVE QUALITIES (who you are)	SKILLS/TALENTS (what you're good at)	INTERESTS/HOBBIES (what you enjoy doing)	VALUES (what you consider most important)
1.	1.	1.	1.
2.	2.	2.	2.
3.	3.	3.	3.
4.	4.	4.	4.
5.	5.	5.	5.

Likes and Dislikes of Jobs:

Review the **THREE** most significant work experiences you've had, including volunteer work if applicable. Then indicate **FIVE** things you have **LIKED** and **DISLIKED** about each job and **WHY**. Please be as **SPECIFIC** as possible. The more detailed you are, the more you will get out of this exercise. Lastly, **CIRCLE** any similar patterns you notice among the jobs you've listed.

Example: I liked the building because it was large, modern and had a lot of windows. I disliked my boss because he/she constantly criticized me.

JOB #1:

WHAT I LIKED ABOUT THIS JOB	WHY?	WHAT I DISLIKED ABOUT THIS JOB	WHY?
1.		1.	
2.		2.	
3.		3.	
4.		4.	
5.		5.	

JOB #2:

WHAT I LIKED ABOUT THIS JOB	WHY?	WHAT I DISLIKED ABOUT THIS JOB	WHY?
1.		1.	
2.		2.	
3.		3.	
4.		4.	
5.		5.	

JOB #3:

WHAT I LIKED ABOUT THIS JOB	WHY?	WHAT I DISLIKED ABOUT THIS JOB	WHY?
1.		1.	
2.		2.	
3.		3.	
4.		4.	
5.		5.	

Take a Trip to the Site of Your Perfect Job:

Here is a fun exercise to help you to picture working at your perfect job. Do this when you are alone in a quiet place with no distractions.

Take a few minutes to get into a relaxed state of mind. To help get you centered, you may want to light a candle or play some soft background music in the form of whatever you may find appealing. For me it's nature sounds or New Age. Close your eyes and take a deep breath, hold it for five seconds and slowly release it. Repeat this a few more times until your body is relaxed and your mind is relatively free from thoughts.

Now imagine you have been transported to the job of your dreams. You can be anywhere you want, doing what you love to do. Complete the following questions by writing the first response that comes to mind. *Please do not censor or put any limitations on your thoughts, as this is a free-flowing exercise and there is no right or wrong way to do this. If you are unable to visualize anything, simply list your preferences after each question.*

Where are you working, geographically?

Do you work indoors or outdoors?

If you work in a building or other structure, what does it look like?

What surrounds it?

What kind of an organization do you work for?

Is it your own business?

Is it a small firm or a large company?

Is the environment formal or informal?

What is the pace? Is it on the quiet side or full of energy?

What are you doing?

Are you on the phone? Working on a PC? Traveling?

Are you working alone or with a team?

Are you working primarily with people, ideas or things?

If you are working with people, are they primarily inside or outside of the organization?

What kind of people are they?

What role do you play? Are you managing others or reporting to a boss?

If you have a boss, what is that boss like?

What are you wearing?

What are your working hours?

How much money do you earn?

You have a folder on your desk with an assignment in it. This is something you will really enjoy doing. What is the assignment?

What do you like most about your job?

What type of recognition do you receive, if any?

What contribution are your making to the organization?

Write down any other thoughts you had or anything else you saw during this exercise.

Choose one word to describe the "essence" or "feeling" of your experience.

How did you do? Don't worry if you got "stuck" on some questions; simply focus on the answers you *did* receive. The point here is to consider all the elements that comprise your working environment and envision them just as you'd wish them to be.

Step 2: Evaluate Your Progress.

What have you learned from doing the exercises?

Based on the results of the exercises, what field(s) do you see yourself exploring further?

Step 3: Research Your Options.

Start to research all fields of interest to determine if they are a good match for you. The four best ways to do this are through the internet, library, volunteer work and informational interviews. While conducting my own career search, each time I met someone who seemed like they had a "great" job, I would ask them questions I wanted to know such as: What do they like most and least about their job? What is a typical day like? What is the entry-level salary? This gave me valuable inside information that led me to either discard or pursue those options.

Step 4: Go For It!

Once you have a clear picture of what you would like to do, the last step is to put it into action. This may be in the form of taking a course on what interests you, transitioning into your ideal work slowly through part-time employment, volunteer work or running full speed ahead into your new career.

The following two success stories may help to inspire you:

A client I've been working with for some time is a Yale graduate who lives in Manhattan. She spent quite a few years in the advertising field, climbing the corporate ladder. When I met her, she had just been laid off from her job and was burnt-out, discouraged and felt "dead" inside. She was so disconnected from herself and her inner wisdom that she had forgotten who she was and what was important to her. Many of our coaching sessions involved completing and discussing exercises such as the ones in this article. She soon re-connected with her lifelong passion and is now successfully pursuing a career in acting and modeling.

I received an e-mail recently from another woman who had attended one of my "Discover Your Ideal Career" workshops. While completing the exercise that required her to list her strengths and talents, she discovered that organizing was her greatest strength. She also knew that she excelled when a project required a vision and a plan to carry it out. In the weeks that followed the workshop, she wondered how she could make a living utilizing this talent. Suddenly it came to her—she would become a professional organizer. She started her business which has taken off just like the hot air balloons she has on her colorful website.

Discovering your ideal career is like climbing a mountain. There are a variety of paths to choose, and the terrain can be rocky, with the peak nowhere in sight. But if you keep pushing ahead with determination and perseverance, when you do finally reach the top you will undoubtedly find that it was worth the journey.

Five Steps For Locating Your Ultimate Profession
Written By Deborah Brown-Volkman

Are you unhappy in your present career? Are you having trouble deciding what to do next? Are there too many choices or not enough direction? Are you looking for a word from above that will show you the way?

There are times in our career when we are at a crossroads. Some of us actively seek our next step, while others wait for the next step to come to them. If you believe you can have a career that will bring you excitement and fulfillment, then you will have that. If you believe that work is work, and it's all about making it to the weekend, then "working for the weekend" will be your reality.

So, How Can Do You Find A Career That Will Bring You Joy and Satisfaction?

Follow These Five Steps:

1. Describe What You Want:

You cannot get what you want until you can describe what it is. What do you want your career to look like? What characteristics are important to you? Answer the following:

During What Part Of The Workday Am I:

1. Most Enthusiastic?

2. Most Content?

3. Most Effective?

4. Most Frustrated?

As you write down what you want, do not forget to consider your career within the context of your overall life plan.

Answer the following questions:

1. Where Do I Want To Be Located?

2. What Industry Do I Want To Work In?

3. How Many Hours Do I Want To Spend Working?

4. How Much Do I Want To Earn?

5. Do I Want To Keep My Current Career Long-term Or Only Until I Transition Into A New Career?

Your goal is to create a picture of your ideal career. Gather your answers in one place and describe exactly what you see yourself doing if there were no obstacles in your way. Do not screen yourself or come up with reasons why it will never work. Do not get bogged down with logistics. Give yourself the freedom to express yourself and declare what you want. This will set the foundation and clarify where you are headed.

Are you waiting for the perfect description? If the answer is yes, you will be waiting a long time. You will never know your perfect move until you make it. You only get an inkling of what you want; a feeling in your gut that tells you which way to go. (Consider yourself lucky to have that much!) Usually we look outward for answers to our questions, when the answers are inside us. They have always been there.

2. Explore Your Options:

What did you learn from Step 1? Did you discover that you described something you have been thinking about for a long time, but are uncertain where to start? Did you come up with a few possible career choices, but are unsure which one to select? Did you come up with a few ideas, but nothing concrete?

Now that you have a description, (or at least an idea of what you want), it is time to dig deeper to find out if your description is valid. The exploratory phase is designed to help you with this. A good place to begin is to talk with people you know (or you don't know) who can give you insight into your ultimate profession. Sources can be found anywhere; friends, family, co-workers, etc. You never know who can help you.

Start with those who are doing what you think you would like to do. Ask them how they got into their field and what you can do to follow in their footsteps. Use contacts you have or those who are recommended and call to request an informational interview. Go for it. You may be surprised by the numbers of 'yes' you receive.

Interacting with the right people is the most important part of the exploratory process, but you must also do your own research. Go to the library, the bookstore, and spend time on the Internet. Find books that describe job titles and job descriptions. Looks for books or web sites that can give you a good idea of what is required in the way of experience and training. Uncover resources that can help you capitalize on your knowledge and experience and turn them into actual careers you can transition into.

Resources that can help you are:

- *Department of Labor's Occupational Outlook Handbook* at http://stats.bls.gov/oco/home.htm The Occupational Outlook Handbook is a nationally recognized source of career information, designed to provide valuable assistance to individuals making decisions about their future work lives. Revised every two years, the Handbook describes what workers do on the job, working conditions, the training and education needed, earnings, and expected job prospects in a wide range of occupations.

- *The Complete Guide for Occupational Exploration: An Easy-To-Use Guide to Exploring over 12,000 Job Titles* at http://www.amazon.com/exec/obidos/ASIN/1563700522/surpassyourdr-20/103-3742296-4260641 As anyone who's gone on the job search knows the sheer abundance of the job titles can make it difficult to find the position that you're looking for. Provides completely revised information that reflects the latest job titles based on interests, experience, skills, and training, this book can super-change your search.

Another great resource for exploring your options is university web sites. Most universities have extensive career sections loaded with information that can be useful for you.

This is a period for being open and for letting the answers come to you. You are exploring new territory and uncharted waters. Be comfortable with feeling uncomfortable. You are creating the next phase of your career.

Once you have a few choices, "pro and con" them to see if they really are a match. Your goal is to find a career that either fits into your current lifestyle, or one that you can transition into. Remember that this is why it is called a transition, because it happens in stages over time.

Take your time, but do not leave this step until you have a pretty good picture of what you want to do next. This stage may be the longest of the exploratory process. Trust that the work you are doing is necessary to take you to where you want to be.

3. Create Your Game Plan:

Once you have your description, and the exploratory process is complete, it is time to go after what you want.

Here are three steps to put into your plan:

a) What Do You Want? Example: I want to change careers, get promoted, or enhance my attitude.

b) When Will Your WHAT Be Achieved? Example: 3 months from now, 6 months, etc? Be specific.

c) How Will You Get There? Take what you gathered from the exploratory process and put these steps into your calendar. You have already found out what you need to do. Now, it's time to make it real.

Items to Include In Your Plan Are:

1. How you will identify the companies you may want to work for. Useful places to locate information can be found at corporate web sites, company news, press releases, local and national newspapers, business and industry journals, and securities and exchange documents.
2. How you will obtain names, addresses, and phone numbers for the person in charge of hiring for the position you are seeking.
3. How you will create a resume and cover letter that matches the position you are researching and how you will send them out.
4. What will be your 30-second pitch that describes the position you want. Your personal commercial will be useful when beginning telephone conversations and follow-up e-mails.
5. How you will tell everyone you know that you are looking for a new position. Who you will network with. What association meetings you will attend to learn more about the industry you are trying to get into and to build your Rolodex.
6. When you will be in your new career. Having something to shoot for will keep you motivated and on track.
7. How you will remind yourself not to give up. At times, you may feel frustrated and discouraged. How will you remind yourself that hard work and persistence will take you to the finish line?

8. How you will be supported. Life is not about reaching our goals alone. Don't make the mistake of thinking you can achieve this by yourself. Ask for help. Let the people in your life assist you.

Your goal is to take each step listed and put your answers down on paper. This will be your roadmap and your plan.

Note: Some Web Sites To Help Facilitate The Exploratory Process Are:

1. American City Business Journals http://www.amcity.com Articles on companies in business publications from cities across the U.S.
2. Business Wire http://www.businesswire.com Business news updated on the hour.
3. Corporate Financials Online http://www.cfonews.com News from some publicly traded companies and 10K and 10Q reports.
4. Corporate Information http://www.corporateinformation.com Information on companies in and outside the U.S., publicly traded or privately held, listed here.
5. Edgar Database of Corporate Information http://www.sec.gov/edgar.shtml Electronic version of documents filed with the U.S. Securities and Exchange Commission. Great source of information.
6. Fortune Magazine http://www.fortune.com Browse this site for information on various companies. Visit the archives to browse past issues back to September 1995.
7. Hoovers.com http://www.hoovers.com Detailed information on companies. You can also access names of top executives within an organization.
8. PR Newswire Company News On-Call http://www.prnewswire.com An online database of stories appearing on PR newswire from participating companies.
9. Public Register's Annual Report Service http://www.prars.com Order your annual reports from this free service. Select from over 3,200 publicly traded companies. You can order online or through a toll-free telephone number.
10. Wall Street Research Net http://www.wsrn.com This site allows you to search for comprehensive information on companies that are publicly traded. You'll be able to access a company description, earnings information, and financials.

4. Implement Your Plan:

This step is about keeping the momentum going no matter what. Set daily, weekly, and monthly goals. Strive to meet them. Persistence and forward movement is what will help you reach your goal.

Implementation is the step when you will carry out the plan you created in Step 3. This is the accountability piece of the process, and it is where most people lose momentum. Each day of the implementation phase should begin with you declaring "Today I will hold myself accountable to my plan." Repeat several times if necessary.

Take the actions on your plan and put them into your calendar. Use the date you selected as your new career deadline and work backwards. What do you have to do by when? Block off chucks of time and specify which actions you will take. If these actions are not written down, there is a very good chance they won't get done.

We all have busy lives, so if you do not make the time for your career to change, your change will not happen. You may have to look at your life and decide if making a change is really important to you now. If it is, then you will have to make the time. A side note: you may have to clear out what is eating up your time. This is a good thing. You may have wanted to address this area for quite some time. This is your opportunity to do so.

Each Sunday evening, sit down with your calendar in front of you. Review your plan and go over what actions you will be taking that week. Write down specifically what you will be doing and how much time you need for each task. Do the same on a daily basis. Each morning, review your calendar and decide what will be done. Reviewing your plan in the morning is the best way to keep it fresh in your mind for the entire day.

Having everything written down in your calendar will make a tremendous difference when you don't feel like doing what you said you would. At times, this step will seem like hard work, and it will feel that way because it is. The difficult part will be battling your excuses and your resistance. This why you created a plan—to overcome your negative thinking and internal objections so the process and your transition would happen.

On some days, you will do everything you said that you would, and some days you will not. Despite your daily declarations, you are not a machine. Life happens and there are unexpected things that crop up that need to be taken care of. It is ok to stray from your plan every once in a while, but if you have stopped completely, it is important to note why. Maybe you are afraid to take the next step? Maybe you don't have enough support? Maybe you are not committed to making the transition at this time. Maybe you need to explore or research more? It is okay to go backwards if it is the catalyst that brings you forward.

Goals are reached one action at a time. If you take one action per day, you will take 30 actions at the end of the month. Your goal is to keep moving no matter what. Persistence and forward movement will take you to your goal.

5. You Reached Your Goal:

This is the step where you get to applaud yourself for all your hard work and effort. You get to be proud of what you accomplished. You made it!

This is the step where you acknowledge yourself for being afraid and going after what you wanted anyway. Not only did this process build character, it made you a happier person.

This is not a time to stand still! I know that my recommendation not to stand still or be complacent may sound contradictory since you have just reached your goal, but your career is something you will have for most of your life. Keep a vision of where you want to see yourself, 5 years, 10 years, or longer in your mind. Your vision will keep you going through the up's and down's of your career. There's more to your career than just the day to day. There is a larger goal and purpose in store for you.

Enjoy today, while planning for tomorrow. You never know what the future will bring, and you want to be prepared. Knowing that you have reached your goal will give you the confidence to take on other goals. Congratulations on discovering that you can handle anything that comes your way.

Teenagers: A Perfect Place For A Choice Career
Written By Grace McAliece

As a teenager you might feel as though everyone else is making decisions for you. You might even feel misunderstood. My question to you is "Do *you* understand you?" Do you spend most of your time either doing what your parents/friends or teachers say, or the opposite? We sometimes end up reacting to people out of emotion, rather than making a choice that best suits us. What would it feel like to make choices that are in our own best interest?

To start making choices it is important to know what you are looking for. Diana Haskins in "Parent as Coach" states that teens are looking for others to: Respect, Listen, Understand, Appreciate, Support, allow them to be Responsible, and help them establish Independence. Would you want any, or all of these? How do you get each of these now? Even when you don't get them as often as you would like there is an alternative. There is a better way. It's about understanding your own needs and filling them. You can give these things to yourself instead of looking for them from other people. Within the following chapter you will be learning how to create a new routine. 'A Perfect Place' is a new way to manifest and maintain your choice life, based on what you value.

Your life purpose is uncovered by what I call, your 'Lifegem.' In other words the answer to your own path in life is the Gem, or wisdom, inside you. I created 'A Perfect Place' for myself, as a reminder to listen to the guidance within me and know the support I do have. Now I am able to stop, ask and listen when I make choices. I no longer go with the flow to get along. It started as a quest to find out what I really want to do with my life. I noticed self-help books had a theme. Certain elements kept coming up for me. As I read I noticed that focusing on the positive, using my intuition, and creating an action plan are all useful things to get what I want. I developed a way to keep me aware, accepting and accountable. I started to notice support that was already there. Now I know I am running my own life with help from the following words: Clear, Near, Hear, Fear, Gear, Adhere and Cheer. I share my own process with my clients and now with you in this chapter.

If you are going to have a winning life, you need to take the wheel. Jay McGraw says in *Life Strategies for Teens*, "...you have to program your life and your world in a way that sets you up for success. That means changing your environment, time schedules, commitments, routines, activities, and objectives."

You are unique and you do make a difference already. How do you want to be viewed or treated? This chapter is intended as a guide to form a nurturing environment to make your own choices. Desired change can happen easily.

As you read this, have fun, be creative and remember this is about the stuff that is supposed to work for you. Following each of these steps are my own examples of how I use 'A Perfect Place.' Try to envision how these steps can be used to develop your own self-understanding and direction.

Step #1: Clear:

Did you ever notice the answer or an idea comes to you when you stop thinking about it? In order to create change it is helpful to erase the chalkboard. Start fresh each day by taking a half an hour to clear. Get away, or step back from everything. Create space to give room for something new. Give space to create. Clear a physical space free from distractions. Create emotional room by letting go of self-judgments and shoulds. Intellectually be open to new ideas. You might think about it like home plate as in baseball. A safe place you cannot be tagged out. This will set the stage to listen to your own inner voice. Mastering this step will allow you to see the big picture by getting away from the details. By being clear you are quiet enough to hear others ideas whether you agree with them or not. This is a huge expression of respect and by showing it you will receive it.

What do you need to be clear? Examples:

- Schedule some time alone (You may even begin to enjoy your own company)
- Take a walk/Bike Ride/Roller blade/Meditate/Journal/Guided Visualizations
- Let go of any expectations or needs (for now)
- Make a physical space at home for yourself
- Take a deep breath when someone says something you don't like

Add yours here:

-
-
-

GEM Examples: I never felt that I knew what I wanted. For one entire summer between 8th and 9th grade, I found myself biking with an old 3-speed bike that was stuck in third gear. I used the time to think about the upcoming change to High school and what I wanted to experience. I rode around the High school to be familiar with the layout. I imagined what I would do if the bigger kids picked on me. I decided to take courses I knew I may never use just for the experience. I participated in many activities like plays, softball, and color guard. Whenever I was sad or hurt I would write poetry. It helped me to sort out my thoughts and feelings. I have since learned how to use 30 minutes each morning to journal. Journaling slows down my active mind, especially when I start worrying about things. I like to call it a brain dump or purging. By not letting my emotions take charge I am able to handle things one step at a time.

Step #2: Near:

Surround yourself with resources. Make note of Encouraging, nurturing people places and things. The stuff you love. This will keep you motivated. Now that you are clear, what will you bring near? Build a foundation of support. Did you ever have a bad start to the day and by concentrating on that more things seemed to go wrong? By focusing on what is working, you will begin to notice more of it. If you have had the experience of being on a baseball team you know that you have a coach, team mates and fans that you can rely on to support you. Certain people, you will notice, are better suited to be open to certain ideas you have. Knowing what and who supports you and mastering the search for it will naturally inspire you. You are learning to hone in on what supports you and to lean on those resources when you need it. How do you support others? What would remind you that you are supported?

What or who, do you want near for support around you? Examples:

- Make a list of nurturing, encouraging people, places and things (Note: Be aware of what is already in place)
- Think of experiences that you enjoy so much you lose track of time
- Brainstorm with someone who will give you permission to explore (without an agenda)
- Gather inspiring pictures/poems/candles (what ever inspires you)
- Join a group of like-minded people sports/clubs or form your own

Add yours here:

-
-
-

GEM Examples: My bike supported me to get away from it all for a while. I painted my room my favorite color, lilac, and that made it more enjoyable for me. I love listening to all kinds of music and how each song can give me a different feeling. My parents and 5 brother and sisters were supportive (Some of the time). My Music teacher (yes a teacher) in high school supported me by taking her own time to teach me more about music and how I can use it to gear up for the future. My teacher suggested with my talents and desires to help people that I should become a Music Therapist. In order to become a Music Therapist I needed to read music and learn an instrument. She took her own time between classes to teach me to sight-read music and she taught my how to play piano. She also gave me the opportunities to give back and not feel that her support was a hand out. She allowed me to help her with school projects and I even helped out by babysitting. My friend and her mother also were supportive by talking about where we would be in the future and what we each wanted to accomplish. To practice Near, I now make a mental list of what supports me and when I can trust someone with certain ideas. I am inspired by nature and love to walk my dog. Ideas or thoughts come to me at these times.

Step #3: Hear:

I hope you noticed a lot of support that surrounds you. This next step is about tapping into your own internal well of resources for the answers. What I mean is your own 'gut' feelings or instinct. In baseball if a player from the other team tells you to run to second base will you? You would look around to see if it's the right thing to do. Start to ask yourself, "Is this the right decision for me or what can I learn from this experience?" Once you are clear and are focused on the support you brought near, what do you hear? How do you want to be treated or viewed? Where are you being guided? What does your intuition say? What do you value? What talents do you have? Once you determine your values, gifts and talents you can use them as a gauge to make choices. Consider your dreams. What might you hear about yourself through them? You have sight, smell, taste, touch and hearing at your disposal. Your body is telling you something through your senses. What might they be telling you? Mastering 'Hear' will give you your own voice, guiding you to what you want to be. By listening to your intuition you will learn to trust your decisions. Other people will listen to your ideas if you express interest in theirs.

What guidance might you use? Examples:

- Practice listening to your Intuition or gut feeling in situations
- Look around and pay attention to what you see, feel or hear
- Search for synchronicity or signs (be patient for an answer, it may come in any form, from an event to something you heard from a friend or TV)
- Pay attention and hear what your body is telling you (butterflies/muscles tensing, what do they mean to you?)
- Write down a detailed description of what you think of when you hear each of the following words: Respect, Listen, Understand, Appreciate, Support, Responsibility, and Independence
- Make a list of your values/Gifts/talents

Add yours here:

-
-
-

GEM Examples: When I reflected on the poems I wrote in High School, I was able to hear that I was getting better at handling my own life. Hanging out on the front porch at my friend's house we shared thoughts of people and life in general. I received an education by listening to what other people experienced and deciding what I would choose in that situation. I have always loved asking other peoples opinions. I always tried to come up with ideas to help people solve problems. I loved inspiring others by talking about how things could be. School tests even showed that I might make a good teacher (Or draftsperson?) I love and have a gift for singing and was encouraged by my music teacher to look into music therapy as a career. I am and have always been in awe about all of life's details and how complex we are. I get a 'hit' or intuition about things sometimes. I might notice or hear something that clicks with what I was thinking about. If it has to do with a choice I am pondering I usually go by that instinct that was confirmed by something someone said or what I saw. As I now write everyday I periodically go back to read my journal. This shows me what affected me and I ask myself what can I do or learn about it or what am I willing to do. My values were determined in my coach training. They happen to match what I had been hearing all my life. My values are Guiding, Inspiring, In Awe, Safety circle (protecting what I value) and Protective.

Step #4: Fear:

Acknowledge fear as it comes up. A fear is real if it's going to affect your moving forward. Let's face it—there are a lot of pressures as a teen. Sometimes we compare ourselves to others who seem to do something easily. We are all at different stages even at the same age. Start from where you are now. What are you willing to do about your fear to get what you want? End the frustration of worrying about where you are supposed to be by asking where do I want to be. Don't get on your own case. Give yourself permission to be where you are in life. What if you believe you are not fast enough, smart enough or strong enough? Understanding fears that block you, will allow you to manage goals accordingly. By knowing your fears you can invent new strategies and still attain the desired outcome. Be patient and creative there are many ways to accomplish the same thing. By being understanding and patient of your own fears, others can learn to understand you.

What are you willing to do about fear? Examples:

- What fear do you notice? Have you experienced it before?
- Work through it with the support you brought near to you. You might want to team up with a life coach to work through your fears
- If you fear a specific step to get your goal try to find another way
- Break it down into manageable steps by listing weekly activities you can do toward your goal

Add yours here:

-
-
-

GEM Examples: One fear I had as a teen was girls are not strong enough. I attempted to disprove that theory. When my Dad would ask my brother to do anything I would always jump in and say "I can do it" just to prove I could. When I was about 15 my brother was asked to move an air conditioner. My brother told my father to ask me. He thought I was stronger than he was. So, I moved through my fear by proving I was strong enough and I gained respect for it. Another fear of mine is traditional schooling. As you will see later I was going to go to college. I backed out because among other things, I feel that I am no good at being tested. About a decade later I dealt with this fear by searching for another way to get training. I then searched for that other way on the Internet. I looked for something that included my skills and talents. Social worker, guidance counselor, and teacher were overlooked right then because of my own fear about school. When I learned about coaching I just knew it was the right thing. I knew it fit just about all of my gifts and talents. At coach training (quite different from traditional school) I learned a lot about myself as well as being a coach.

Step #5: Gear:

You are in a supportive, clear space and giving yourself permission to move forward. Is there something on the list in the 'Hear' section that you want? To 'Gear' up means to prepare yourself to take action. For example if you want 'independence' think of how you have been independent before. What did you do to accomplish this task? For example in baseball there are steps to gear up for in order to get to 2nd base. You know and are prepared for certain things to take place; 1) hit the ball and drop the bat 2) run to 1st base 3) tag 1st base 4) run to 2nd base 5) avoid being tagged out by the 2nd baseman 6) tag the base and stay on 2nd base 7) hear the cheers from your teammates and the crowd. Depending on what the other team does and other circumstances you might have to change your strategy. What you geared up for will give you a shot at getting to 2nd base. Each plan you follow through with will be building independence. Devise a plan as to how you wish to accomplish what you want. This is your project your way. This becomes your goal. Think of the steps that you can gear up for. Take responsibility for the steps to your goal. Take your own path to independence. What do you want and how do you want to get there. By taking steps toward a goal you are proving to yourself and others that you are indeed independent.

What will you need, to gear up for this goal? Examples:

- Visualize your future and write it down in detail
- Create an action plan by asking yourself three questions 1. Where am I now? 2. Where do I want to be? And 3. How am I willing to get there?
- Now break it down into steps you are going to take
- Set a comfortable schedule for completing each step

Add yours here:

-

-

-

GEM Examples: Gearing up with support from my music teacher was easy. I geared up for school. I had, originally, chosen a college and figured out everything I needed to get in. I geared up by putting all of the credentials in place. I visited colleges, studied and took the SAT's, practiced and auditioned with two Italian songs. I was accepted to college. However, for financial fears and my fears around traditional schooling, I chose to gear up for a job, instead. I have decided now not to have my own business because I am not willing to gear up for all that is involved with that. I am now looking to work for a school or organization where I will be able to coach teens. This way there are fewer steps to gear up for and I can work with others, whose values are similar, to gear up for my priority goals.

Step #6: Adhere:

You are on a roll now. In this chapter you have been gearing up for a 'perfect place.' A sort of emotional environment you decide will be best for you to get what you want. How will you stick to your plan? When you start to change course other factors in your life are affected. People may expect the old you and that might elicit self-doubt creating another fear of uncertainty. It might take a while for it to stick. Meanwhile you might want to think of ways to stay devoted to your plan. Doing what you have been doing is easier because you're used to it. Can you carry out your plan and be accountable (face the music or answer to the consequences)? The unexpected may detour you along your path as well. When you hit a pop-up in baseball you just don't know what is going to happen on the way to first base so you run it out full steam ahead as if you had a base hit. What would allow you to 'run it out' or stay the course? By adhering you are expressing responsibility for your own choice life and others will trust you to handle more responsibilities.

What would help you to adhere to what you geared up for? Examples:

- If you feel stuck go back to 'Clear', what do you 'Hear' now?
- Keep the big picture (goal) in mind
- Write reminders to stay on your path; Put them in your notebook or somewhere you will see them often
- Consider using your support systems; who or what will hold you accountable (face the music or answerable)?
- Restructure the timeline of your plan; if you can't do it in one week when can you do it?

Add yours here:

-
-
-

GEM Examples: As a teenager I took advantage of the fact that most of the work to accomplish things were already done. School had organized activities and events that made it easy to participate. I merely chose what sport or activity I wanted to participate in. Practice and games, for softball, rehearsals, for plays and choir were planned by the school. All I had to do was be committed and show up to practice. As an adult now, I adhere by either working with another coach, or telling someone supportive what I am working on. This keeps me on my toes and committed. I adhere by taking comfortable steps so I don't get overwhelmed and give up. I make choices in my life that help me adhere to my plan. I balance my life between what I have to do financially with what I wish to accomplish personally. I support myself financially in a temporary position four days a week thus giving me an extra day for my coaching plan. I visualize working with teens and that inspires me to keep moving forward. I have painted my values on a butterfly mirror. I have it hanging up at home and when I have a decision to make I look at the mirror and ask myself, "Is this decision consistent with my values." I place coaching projects in front of me one after another.

Step #7: Cheer:

Just look at what you have done. Home run! Isn't your life grand? Hey we've got birthdays, graduations and weddings. They all serve to make accomplishments special occasions. Consider celebrating smaller things as well. Treat yourself to something special. Appreciate and maintain awareness of what you are accomplishing. Acknowledge yourself for when you are respectable. Cheer when you make a change and you stick to it (it can be scary to buck your current reality). Cheering is a wonderful way to keep momentum. Write down your actions in case you forget that you can and have done it before. Appreciation is a great motivator. Giving yourself a thank you is wonderful energy to thrive in. Give yourself a pat on the back and take great pride.

What ways might you cheer? Examples:

- Give yourself a gold star
- Write down all accomplishments on a continuing list (it could be a great bio or resume someday.)
- Be in awe of the process of life and the chance to be who you wish to be
- Give thanks to yourself and support system
- Treat yourself to something you enjoy

Add yours here:

-
-
-

GEM examples: In gym class of 9th grade we worked with weights. I ended up beating the whole class, girls and boys, for pumping the most weight on the leg press. This was as a direct result of the strength I gained from bike riding in third gear. Students and teachers cheered me. One teacher, who chose to acknowledge only the strength of the boys, not only appreciated my strength but also asked me to go out for track. As an adult now, I cheer for the steps I've taken by treating myself to stuff like books, time for TV or I make a list of things to cheer about. Once a week I share these accomplishments with a coaching group that was formed to keep us all on track as coaches. The bigger accomplishments such as writing an article or speaking to a group go on my resume adding to what my experience is. By writing and reflecting on what I've done I see a pattern develop. For example I noticed I write longer and more passionately when it's about teenagers. My direction or path appeared and as a coach, I see who I want to work with.

The best personal example of tying these steps together would be how I decided on a new career path. I spent a week totally alone without TV or radio. I thought about all the support I did have and, decided not to share my thoughts with anyone until I had made a firm decision myself. The book "The Celestine Prophecy" supported me. I used it as a guide and worked through the exercises. From the exercises in the book and reflecting, I made a list of all my talents and what I was drawn to. With the list I searched the Internet. I kept in mind my fears of not testing well in school and not wanting to spend too much time or money. Then I read about Coaching and it fit my talents and addressed my fears. The organization I selected was five days in person and six months on the phone once a week. I could certainly spare that time requirement and the in person training was not at a school but someone's home and I felt very comfortable with that. I geared up for school that September. To cut down on cost I shared a room with someone else from training. I arranged for three participants for practice sessions required by the training program. I adhered by writing in a calendar a schedule of when to study and make the teleclass calls. I cheer by having a butterfly mirror (the same mirror with my values) with life coach on one wing and lifegem on the other. This mirror represents my commitment to my values and to the coaching profession.

And that completes the general steps to creating your own Perfect Place. What do *you need* to implement these steps? Practice the ideas you wrote after the examples. If what you first thought of does not work, you can try something else. This is a place you are creating for your own on-going support.

A Perfect Place is a gentle and easy way to remember that which you are learning about yourself. A way of keeping awareness, acceptance and accountability. Be consistant with your choice of accomplishing each step. When you give yourself these gifts you might start to notice it from others. Respect, support, listen, understanding, independence, responsibility, and appreciation will be yours. If your path is left to others how will you get there?

A friend asked me once what my dream was. I didn't know how to answer. I never really thought about what I wanted. I did not have a dream or a goal to work for. After several years of self-help books and much thought about what I really wanted, I finally have a dream. I gear up for each step I feel I need to take toward that dream. In this chapter I have shared the steps I used to get here. Use the words Clear, Near, Hear, Fear, Gear, Adhere and Cheer as cues to assure that you are covering all of the bases. Making any future decisions in this space is easy once you make it a habit. As you move forward in your 'Perfect Place' you will begin to see your own goals more clearly. Learn about what is most important to you. Stay devoted to what you value in life. Dr. Phil McGraw (author Jay McGraw's Dad) uses the phrase "Stand for something or you'll fall for anything." What do you stand for and what steps will you take toward it now?

Always remember that you are Respectable, Listened to, Understood, Appreciated, Supported, Responsible, and Independent. My hope is that by being aware of all of your assets you will experience the encouragement and support needed to have a winning life.

Instructions:

Complete the following. When done, hang it up in your 'Clear' space at home. Use this Quick Guide as a gentle reminder to assure you are accounting for each step of your perfect place. Practice each step starting with 'Clear'. Look at the examples we discussed. For one week play with how you will accomplish this task. Each succeeding week add the next step until you get each mastered on a regular basis. You will be able to recite Clear, Near, Hear, Fear, Gear, Adhere, Cheer and they will prompt you to account for it.

Perfect Place For a Choice Life

Query—How you want to be viewed or treated?

Clear/Week 1—The space you create to detach from outside stuff.

Near/Week 2—People, places and things that support you, unconditionally.

Hear/Week 3—Your ability to hear your inner voice.

Fear/Week 4—Your ability to to recognize fear or a block and work through or around.

Gear/Week 5—Make a plan to accomplish your goal.

Adhere/Week 6—Things that will keep you on track or hold you accountable.

Cheer/Week 7—Ways of memorializing your accomplishments.

Parents: Helping Youngsters Choose A Career
Written By Siegmundo Hirsch

The more children learn who they are, the assets they have, and what the labor market may be like in the future, the higher the probability that they can plan and prepare for a more fulfilling life.

Youngsters 16 years old and above can learn much about themselves by taking *in-depth* aptitude, interest, motivational, values, skills, and personality assessments. Many are free or relatively inexpensive; some can be found in books, on-line, or in a career counselor's office. The three samples provided are a compendium of similar instruments. They focus on values, skills and personality strengths.

Work-Related Values Assessment:

Instructions: This checklist mentions some of the values that people regard as important in finding satisfaction. Values are the things that a person holds dear. Please read each item carefully and put a checkmark next to those that are important to you, or that you feel would be important to have in a future job. When you are done, go back over the list and put a second checkmark beside the six items that you consider the most important. Finally, summarize the results at the end of this instrument.

ACHIEVEMENT: Attaining mastery of a field, self-advancement, growth.
ADVENTURE: Working in a job that requires taking risks.
ALTRUISM: Devotion to the service to others.
AUTHORITY: Working in a job in which you use your position to control others.
CHALLENGE: Handling difficult or complex work.
COMPETITION: Working in a job in which you compete with others.
COWORKERS: Contact with colleagues that promotes a sense of belonging.
CREATIVITY AND SELF-EXPRESSION: Working in a job in which you use your imagination to find new ways to do or say something.
FLEXIBLE WORK SCHEDULE: Working in a job where you choose the work hours.
HELPING OTHERS: Working in a job in which you provide direct services to persons with problems.
HIGH SALARY: Working in a job where many workers earn a large amount of money.

INDEPENDENCE: Working in a job in which you decide for yourself what work to do and how to do it.

INFLUENCING OTHERS: Working in a job in which you influence the opinions or decisions of others.

INTELLECTUAL STIMULATION: Working in a job which requires a considerable amount of thought and reasoning.

INTERPERSONAL RELATIONS: Being with other employees, colleagues.

LEADERSHIP: Working in a job in which you direct, manage, or supervise the activities of others

MORAL VALUES: Behaving in a way consistent with some moral code.

OUTSIDE WORK: Working out-of doors.

PHYSICAL WORK: Working with your hands or bodily strength.

PRESTIGE: Working in a job which gives you status and respect in the community.

PUBLIC ATTENTION: Working in a job in which you have daily dealings with the public.

RECOGNITION: Working in a job in which you gain public notice.

RESEARCH WORK: Working in a job in which you follow established procedures requiring little change.

SEASONAL WORK: Working in a job where you are employed only at certain times of the year.

SECURITY: Work that is stable and relatively free from turnover.

SOCIAL WELFARE: Doing something that benefits other people.

SUPERVISORY RELATIONS: Work done under a fair, agreeable, and professionally nurturing boss.

TRAVEL: Working in a job in which you take frequent trips.

VARIETY: Working in a job in which your duties change frequently.

WORK WITH CHILDREN: Working in a job where you teach or otherwise care for children.

WORK WITH HANDS: Working in a job in which you use your hands or hand tools.

WORK WITH MACHINES OR EQUIPMENT: Working in a job in which you use machines or equipment.

WORK WITH NUMBERS: Working in a job in which you use mathematics or statistics.

SUMMARY: MY TOP WORK-RELATED VALUES ARE:

Work Value #1 _____

Work Value #2 _____

Work Value #3 _____

Work Value #4 _____

Work Value #5 _____

Work Value #6 _____

Related to values is the matter of skills, whether already acquired or to be learned. Which of these are meaningful to your child?

Skills Assessment:

Instructions: Please check off the skills that you are proficient at or that you would like to develop and use on a job. Read each item carefully and put a checkmark next to those that are important to you, or that you feel would be important to have in the future. When you are done, go back over the list and put a second checkmark beside the ten items that you consider the most important. Next, summarize the results at the end of this instrument.

ADMINISTRATIVE/SUPPORT SKILLS

Assisting
Compiling/comparing
Computer literacy
Detail follow-up
Dispatching
Executing
Expediting
Following instructions
Following up
Getting things done
Implementing decisions
Office management
Recording
Record keeping
Scheduling
Supporting key person(s)

MANAGEMENT SKILLS

Administration
Attention to follow-up
Budgeting/Resource allocation
Coaching/developing others
Consulting others
Delegating
Decision making
Establishing management systems
Information management
Job design
Meeting & committee management
Mentoring
Monitoring
Motivating
Effecting strategic objectives
Performance appraisal

PLANNING SKILLS

Anticipating problems
Assigning
Designing
Detail work
Developing
Follow up
Hiring
Inventing
Managing
Organizing
Recommending
Redesigning
Scheduling
Setting goals

Persuading
Planning/Organizing
Priority setting
Problem Solving
Staffing (Hiring/Firing/Promoting)
Systems establishment
Team building
Technology management
Time management
Trouble shooting

LEADERSHIP SKILLS

Agenda setting
Change management
Communicating goals/visions
Crisis management
Cultivating networks
Empowering others
Environmental scanning
Establishing goals/objectives
External. relations
Policy making
Risk assessment
Strategic planning
Strategy management
Values building
Vision/foresight

PERSUASION/SELLING SKILLS

Advocating
Arbitrating/Mediating
Bartering
Conflict Resolution
Convincing
Debating
Developing rapport
Establishing credibility
Fund raising

COMMUNICATION SKILLS

Answering questions
Chairing meetings
Consulting
Editing/p roofing
Giving feedback
Giving speeches
Worming
Instructing/teaching
Interviewing

Manipulating
Marketing
Mobilizing
Motivating
Negotiating
Promoting
Reasoning
Reconciling
Recruiting
Selling

Languages
Letter writing
Listening
Public relations
Report writing
Speaking
Speech writing
Summarizing
Translating
Writing

HELPING SKILLS

Advising
Answering questions
Assisting
Attending
Coaching
Consoling
Counseling
Delivering
Establishing rapport
Hosting
Influencing
Liaison
Listening
Mentoring
Motivating
Providing
Referring
Representing others
Servicing
Soothing
Tact/diplomacy
Understanding

PERFORMING SKILLS

Acting
Dancing
Demonstrating
Entertaining
Leading
Lecturing
Making presentations
Modeling
Moderating
Public speaking
Singing
Telling jokes

MANUAL SKILLS

Machine operation
Manual dexterity
Mechanical reasoning
Model building
Object Assembly
Precision work
Repairing
Word processing

CREATIVE/ARTISTIC SKILLS

Color sense
Conceptualizing

RESEARCH/ANALYTICAL SKILLS

Analyzing
Classifying

Composing
Creating ideas
Creating/developing programs
Creating/developing materials
Decorating
Designing
Drafting
Drawing
Facilities/structural design
Interior design
Landscape design
Mapping
Photography
Playing instruments
Restoring
Shaping materials
Staging presentations/performances
Styling
Visualizing end product
Writing (many varieties)

Conceptualizing
Computer skills:
   accessing data
   analyzing data
   programming
   systems analyses
Evaluating data
Financial & Quantitative analysis
Forecasting
Inquiring
Inspecting
Interviewing
Investigating
Planning
Problem identification
Problem-solving
Recognizing needs
Research design
Surveying
Synthesizing data

NUMERICAL SKILLS

Accounting
Allocating
Appraising
Auditing
Bookkeeping
Budget reviews
Calculating
Computing
Cost analysis
Developing budgets
Estimating
Financial analysis
Keeping records
Math skills
Number memory
Projecting

HANDS ON/PHYSICAL SKILLS

Athletics/sports
Driving
Good sense of hearing Good sense of hearing
Growing things Growing things
Keen eyesight
Landscaping
Navigating
Organizing
Physical coordination
Survival skills
Swimming
Traveling
Walking
Working with animals

Rapid use of numbers
Reporting
Spreadsheet analysis
Statistical work
Taking inventory
Inventing

INNOVATING SKILLS

Applied research
Developing
Experimenting
Generating ideas
Imagining

Relating abstract ideas
Solving problems
Synthesizing

Summary: The Ten Skills That I Would Like To Use The Most Are:

1. .... 2. ....

3. .... 4. ....

5. .... 6. ....

7. .... 8. ....

9. .... 10. ....

After further exploration you will be able to find educational and career options that will allow you to use a combination of these skills. Having clarified your child's values, skills and career orientation, are they consistent with his or her personality? Here is an easy way to find out:

Personality Strengths Assessment:

It is important that your youngster know his or her strengths; it's an opportunity to enhance self image, sense of uniqueness and begins to shape a sense of future direction.

Instructions: To help sharpen your focus, please work through this checklist of personal characteristics. As you proceed, try to recognize all the qualities you possess—irrespective of whether they have been expressed in your educational or work experience so far.

First, read each word and underline the ones that describe you as you are today.

Second, look back over the list, and check off the words that are most highly descriptive of you.

Third, list the ten items that are the most meaningful to you at the end of this instrument.

Please evaluate yourself with kindness. There are no right or wrong answers; only honest ones that will reveal all that is special and unique about you.

academic	dignified	loyal	retiring
active	discreet	mature	robust
accurate	dominant	methodical	self-confident
adaptable	eager	meticulous	self-controlled
adventurous	easygoing	mild	sensible
affectionate	efficient	moderate	sensitive
aggressive	emotional	modest	serious
alert	energetic	natural	sincere
ambitious	fair-minded	obliging	sociable
artistic	farsighted	open-minded	spontaneous
attractive	firm	opportunistic	spunky
bold	flexible	original	stable
broad-minded	forceful	outgoing	steady
businesslike	formal	painstaking	strong
calm	frank	patient	strong-minded
capable	friendly	peaceable	sympathetic
careful	generous	persevering	tactful
cautious	gentle	pleasant	teachable
charming	good-natured	poised	tenacious
cheerful	healthy	polite	thorough
clear-thinking	helpful	practical	tolerant
clever	honest	precise	tough
competent	humorous	progressive	trusting
competitive	idealistic	prudent	trustworthy
confident	imaginative	purposeful	unaffected
conscientious	independent	quick	unassuming
conservative	individualistic	quiet	understanding

considerate	informal	rational	unexcitable
cool	intellectual	realistic	uninhibited
cooperative	intelligent	reflective	verbal
courageous	inventive	relaxed	versatile
curious	kind	reliable	warm
caring	leisurely	reserved	wholesome
deliberate	likeable	resourceful	wise

Summary: My Top Ten Personality Strengths Are:

1. .... 2. ....

3. .... 4. ....

5. .... 6. ....

7. .... 8. ....

9. .... 10. ....

It is to the advantage of youngsters to be encouraged to explore the things, activities and ideas that they like, and exposed to the broad array of options they'll have, as they mature, to express these talents and passions in a profession or life choice.

Parents also can encourage their children to communicate clearly and concisely, and see to it that they acquire good study habits. For example: encourage writing, speaking and reading, and by means of tutors and involvement in community assistance programs.

By being exposed to a variety of people and circumstances, youngsters will be encouraged to develop their emotional intelligence; relating well to others will foster respect, adaptability, creativity, sensitivity and empathy. They also can be introduced to contending with ambiguity; for instance, by discussing relevant news stories, and how different people approach developments from multiple moral and practical perspectives. They can be asked to overcome age-appropriate problems and to solve puzzles they want others to handle for them, and invited to challenge their parents regarding questions of their choice.

The value of positive feedback cannot be exaggerated. As long as their exploration is reasonable and safe, encourage initiative. Children respond well when praised for trying new things. And, even when they are contending with failure and disappointment, youngsters gain from a quiet and friendly discussion of what might have been done differently.

The ground for sound educational and professional decisions begins to be tilled early. Children develop a strong self-image when they find validation in the words and deeds of those who care for them. It eases their way into the future. It is the parents' best legacy.

Chapter Five:
Building A Successful Business

Creating Your Business Environment for a Different Kind of "Green"
Written By Andrea Feinberg

In the last 35 years, both awareness and concern for our natural environment have become part of our consciousness. Natural fibers, recycling, biodegradable goods, concern for natural habitats, the disappearing ozone layer, and second-hand smoke are all concepts that have filtered into our personal and business behaviors. The result of this awareness is a pretty good understanding of the interdependence we have with our natural environments and reasons to respect them. I wouldn't be surprised if you told me you examine labels on your purchases to determine that they meet your standards for 'environmentally sound'.

I wonder—do you have a similar appreciation for the contribution of your working environments to your business success? I mean, do you appreciate *the relationship between the environment in which you and your employees work and an ability to be creative and productive while working?* Do you understand the many ways in which you can create an environment that fosters important business qualities—loyalty, enthusiasm, desire to contribute, creativity and productivity—both for yourself and, if you have them, employees?

I'm sure you remember the popular debate about nature vs. nurture—the impact of genetic heritage vs. the environment in shaping who we are, our values, behaviors and attitudes. Current thinking is that environment wins this contest. Whether that's true is irrelevant. What *is* important is that environment has been displayed to have a huge impact on our personal attributes—who we are, what we believe, how we feel, and the attitudes and expectations we display towards others.

We rarely think about this, I'm sure, yet we all inhabit a variety of "environments" that affect our business life. Some are obvious—for example, we know that if we're cold, in the dark and hungry, work is not likely to be at the top of our priorities while in that environment of physical deprivation. Some other environments are not so obvious yet they have considerable impact, just the same. And, if they are not consciously designed and nurtured, our working environments can have a major impact on our business success, affecting our ability to attract and keep desirable employees, maintain attendance, creativity, productivity; foster good work habits, team effectiveness, use of time, valuable communications—essentially all those qualities and habits your business depends on to get the job done. If you're a solo-preneur, all these qualities that you depend upon within yourself can be enhanced or stymied by the environments in which you work.

I say 'environments', plural, because there's much more than the furniture to consider. I'm sure you've experienced this. Consider these two examples: You walk into a new restaurant with which you confirmed a reservation. You're greeted with a smile, your reservation is noted, there's pleasing music but not so loud as to compete with conversation. You're told it'll take a few minutes to prepare your table and, in the meantime you're given menus to review and offered a beverage from the bar. Within minutes, the host finds you, apologizes for the wait and escorts you to a nicely set table with a hope you'll enjoy your meal. Your expectation for the rest of the dining experience is for a great evening. Now let's walk into another new establishment for which a reservation was made. Upon entering, you hear overwhelmingly loud music, find the host arguing with a waiter and not acknowledging your presence. When he finally turns to you, without apology or greeting, he makes no eye contact, does not acknowledge your reservation, leads you to a table that has not yet been cleared, walks you back to the entry to await clean up with other restless, hopeful diners and provides neither a place to sit nor a menu. Looking forward to the meal?

In these cases, the environment was created by a combination of features, including sounds, behavior, a concern (or not) for your satisfaction, pride in appearance (or not!). And, because this kind of business deals with retail customers, both employees and customers were affected by their environment.

This may not be the kind of business in which you find yourself so let's review other features contributing to a working environment that may be more relevant for you, such as proximity and access to:

- information
- a current or outdated level of technology
- training
- music
- acknowledgement
- opportunity
- sociability
- art
- a sense of contribution

Like a tasty stew, there are many individual ingredients that, when combined, create a unique and distinct working 'flavor'. Take any one away and the experience changes. Have a particular flavor in mind—zesty, mild, sweet, tart? Then you'll test the ingredients and their level of contribution each step of the way as you're preparing for the outcome—a tasty meal. And so it is in your working environment. *The more care and awareness we put into the environments in which we work, the greater likelihood we'll have of directing the outcomes of our work.*

Let's spend a moment with this point. While I know some people work for the love of the process and activity, I'm guessing you work to create a specific outcome—it could be your sense of freedom, maybe it's to achieve your idea of wealth and success. It could even be that working is your opportunity to contribute to society, charity, the planet. Whatever is your desired outcome, as a business owner or manager, I know you spend enormous amounts of time, energy and money working to make it happen. By paying attention to the many environments in which all this effort is expended, you'll have a greater ability to guide your business, including the contribution you expect from your staff, to your desired outcomes. And, perhaps more importantly, by designing working environments that are consistent with your desired outcome there will be far less struggle to make it happen. *The appropriate environments for a given outcome become an asset in your business plan.*

OK, enough from me. This is your opportunity to reflect and act upon what's meaningful for you in your place of business. I'm going to ask you to commit to paper the answers to the following questions. You may intuitively know the answers already but haven't really acknowledged the direct impact they have on your effective working habits. So please write them down. Doing so will bring your awareness to a more conscious place in your brain and help you see where you have choice—choice in shifting those environmental factors to enhance or reduce their impact on your business and, if you've got them, employees. Reflecting upon your relevant situation and writing down your answers will help you to replicate the best possible circumstances for the outcome you desire of all your hard work applied to your business. If you don't have employees, this is an ideal opportunity to enhance your own working space with tools you need to be more effective.

1. Physical space:

Earlier, I mentioned the example of physical workspace as having an impact on your ability to work effectively. Having good light, comfortable seating, necessary tools, appropriate air flow and temperature seems obvious to your ability to work well, doesn't it? And who can concentrate over a grumbling tummy? I'm sure you offer these necessities to yourself or those who work on your behalf. Now, please turn your attention inward for a moment. What might be some less obvious but equally important components to help you or employees work comfortably and effectively? Many of us use art, plants or favorite toys to liven up a workspace. Just ask yourself this question: where are you when you're doing your best work? If it's your working space you're lucky. Wherever it is, *what's in that space that's so supportive of your business activity?* Colors you enjoy? Music that pleases you? Photos that evoke your personal life, hobbies or passions? Comfortable furniture? Access to others? Solitude? Here we go:

Reflect and Act:

1) Where are you when performing at your best? Creating your best work?

2) Why? What's happening? What are you responding to? What do you see or feel that helps this to happen?

3) Are you more or less productive at varied times during your usual work day?

4) What personally meaningful amenities have you given yourself to enhance your working space? For example—favorite music, personal photos, an inspiring piece of art, souvenirs and so forth?

5) Why do these specific items work for you? How do you feel as a result of having them in your workspace, a feeling you wouldn't experience if they were gone?

Now that you've considered the small yet personally meaningful, shift over to the larger shared spaces that communicate to you or your employees how they are valued by the 'business':

1) What is the condition of the company parking lot? Is it well-lit? Swept? Plowed?

2) If there is no parking lot, do employees have a safe place to keep their cars? If driving is not the norm for your area, consider how employees get to work—is it safe, timely, reasonably priced? Can you contribute to any improvements in these options?

3) Will you reimburse employees for their travel over some basic minimum monthly expense?

4) What is the condition of the bathrooms? The shared or private spaces such as a cafeteria, stairwells or elevator? Using the space provided, please write which ones are serving to enhance your employees' desire to work well on your behalf? Which spaces are putting up barriers to that outcome?

5) What specifically *are* the barriers? For example, are bathrooms cleaned, well lit with amenities such as fresh soaps, towels, flowers? Are stairs in good working order, swept and with open doors?

6) What can you do to improve these situations and when will that be accomplished?

Did you learn something here? If you've acknowledged that there are specific items, places or times of day that enhance your desire to work well, is there a way to offer a similar opportunity to employees? If you've discovered you enjoy working at home vs. working in your place of business, is there something from your home you can replicate in your place of business to augment that experience? If you know the things you have in your working space that support your business activity, have you offered the same opportunity to your employees? If you do your best work when out of the office, how can you bring to your office those touches that embrace your work habits?

Now consider the impact of a working social culture, the general 'people environment' that's evident in every business. Let's look at this example: a company that discourages communication with colleagues and provides no company-wide communication device, provides no regular access to management, requires employees to document working time in 1/2 hour increments, provides minimal reward or acknowledgement for desirable results, provides none for attempts that didn't work out as planned, will not reimburse training or learning opportunities, is rigid about being in the office and does not encourage taking new approaches to solve problems. Sound like a fun place to try new ideas? Be innovative? Be committed to the corporate mission? *If the social aspects of your business environment are not willing to support your employees with these forms of encouragement and acknowledgment, why would those employees be willing to support you?*

We can think about this another way. When we're developing pet projects, don't we bend over backwards to give them all the support we can to ensure they'll succeed and thrive? We find funds to develop and promote them, we find champions who'll support their development, we find partners, test markets, affiliates and more. Just as you would provide this sort of supportive 'environment' for a new pet project or service, every working person deserves all the support available to ensure success—success for themselves and for the contribution they make to your business. Part of this support comes from the environments in which we all work.

Consider all the elements your business possesses that serve to create an environment. This environment is like a garment that cloaks your employees when they come to work and it affects their comfort, willingness, and energy. The physical and intangible features of your business all convey a message and, whether subtle or overt, they're guiding the outcomes of your efforts, perhaps not in the direction you'd like them to go. So it makes sense to identify what those features are, determine if they're aiding or detracting from your desired business outcomes and find a way to shift them for maximum benefit—for you, your employees and your business. Consider these and how they affect your business:

2. Relationships:

The general social culture in which we work has a huge impact on influencing behaviors, guiding us to fit in or feel odd, resistant. Our colleagues, managers, employees, and associates—the people with whom we have regular contact— create *an environment of attitude*, either supporting or defeating our efforts to complete tasks. Are you likely to try something new, submit an initiative, follow through on a pet project, volunteer your ideas if those around you are negative, denigrating, rude and unappreciative? Do you think similar attitudes affect the degree of interest your employees have in doing excellent work? In wanting to do more than the minimum required? You bet they do.

On the other hand, an environment of support, regular feedback, appreciation, ongoing communication, and encouragement for contribution can be created with little cost and huge payback for your business.

<u>Reflect and Act:</u>

1) What is the last comment that was said to you about you or your work that put you on Cloud 9 for the rest of the day? When was the last time a comment you offered provided the same result?

2) Have employees? How often do you check in with them to see how things are going?

3) Does your company newsletter keep staff informed about current and planned activities? Does it ask for their ideas and comments? Does it publicly acknowledge initiatives and achievements they've made? What is the downside if these things are not in place? The upside to having them?

4) What one personal thing do you know about each employee who works for you? What do you know, personally, about colleagues that would help express an appropriately positive interest in them each day? If you don't have employees, apply this to vendors, networking partners and colleagues.

5) Does each employee know you want them to contribute to this business in their own unique way? What 3 things can you do to best promote and ensure that awareness?

6) When you meet with employees or team members to follow up on projects that didn't work as expected, is there a tone of blame or do you make it clear you want to understand what went wrong to improve the process for next time?

7) Which of the previous behaviors is more likely to ensure there will be a 'next time'? How can you make this work best for employees and the business?

8) What are your human resource policies on benefits, advancement, training opportunities, awards, performance reviews? How often do you review these personnel policies? What measurements are used to determine these policies are effective for the business?

9) Does everyone know about these policies? If not, what opportunities are you missing? What one thing can you do to change this situation today? Within 30 days? One year from today?

3. Networks:

These are our customers, partners, web relations, the '6-degree' circle of associates we all possess. What we know, who we know and how well we share our knowledge, contacts and tips create *an environment of value.* Possessing a mentality of abundance (a willingness to share, knowing that by giving you get in return, believing that others' success can be your success) creates a reputation for you of great value. A mentality of scarcity (believing that there's not enough to go around, that shortage creates value, that fear is a great motivator) is far less likely to reap you the true rewards of networking: being let into the enormous webs of valuable connections represented by all those business cards exchanged at monthly business meetings, luncheons and seminars.

Reflect and Act:

1) What's your goal when attending a networking function? (If it's to collect business cards, may I ask you to try something new? At your next networking function, focus all attention on the party with whom you're speaking. Think—who do you know who could help this person? Who do you know who could use this person's expertise? And, finally, who does this person know who could help others in your circle? In other words, don't consider at all the likelihood that this person might buy from you. Instead, try focusing entirely on offering assistance; see if this results in a different level of networking success for you)

2) When was the last time you shared information or a tip with someone without expectation of return?

3) How often have you put 2 people together who could benefit each other without assuming a reward of any kind?

4. Our Self:

This category of environment includes our health, personal gifts, values, energy, the attitude with which we face the world. We know that when we don't feel well, physically, we simply are less likely to produce our best work. We're easily defeated by a cold, summer or otherwise. The same can happen if we're doing work that doesn't take advantage of, or worse, denigrates our personal skill set or our values. For example, I love to write and interact with people in business conversation; if I had a job that didn't allow me to do either I'd express far less passion for the work than if I could express myself through those activities I most enjoy. Or think how difficult it can be to produce quality work if you're in an environment that contradicts your values. If you (or your employees) have to check your sense of integrity at the door each morning, you're coming to work with an important component missing.

<u>Reflect and Act</u>

1) Does your place of business provide an environment in which employees are supported to do their best work for you?

2) Take a look at the way your employees perform and step up to the plate; are they engaged in tasks, on your behalf, that maximize the skills, gifts and strengths they could be contributing for you? Which employee might be better suited in a shifted role? A new department? With a new partner or team? And, most importantly, *how do you know or how will you find out?* Can you commit to making this assessment over the next 30 days?

3) Do you know the true strengths of each employee? If you have no employees, do you understand your own? Are those gifts engaged in service to your business?

4) Are you or your employees encouraged to maintain professional affiliations that will increase their effectiveness for your business?

5) Are they informed about opportunities to learn, to read materials you make available to keep them up to speed on changes in your industry?

6) Do you know specifically why they—your employees—work for you and whether you can enhance that reward for them?

7) Are your personnel policies supportive of their personal lives? In what way are they? In what way can you make improvements? What improvements can you make over the next 24 hours that will put your policies on the path to supporting your employees' (or your own) personal lives?

8) Does your business support any charitable or socially responsive activity? How might doing so affect your business or the quality of work contributed by employees? How can you select a socially conscious commitment that involves or empowers your employees?

Creating an environment that supports your business may be trickier than just providing the necessary physical tools and working space but it doesn't have to be costly. It calls for taking a look at the messages your employees get from all the environments in which they operate on your behalf and ensuring those messages say *'you and your work are valued and vital to the health of this business; how can we support you toward that goal?'* And, depending upon the style in which you want your business to thrive, different environments may be suitable. For example, what would work in your place of business if your working style is collaborative? Intra-preneurial? Contemplative? Brain-storming? Tele-commuting?

You may wonder: when is the ideal time to commit to making those changes that will realize a vision of supportive working environments? That's easy: it's _now_. The moment you realize that what you want to offer in your place of business is not what's there currently—the moment you realize that you could have much more support for all the work you do from the people you already have on board to direct your desired outcomes from working—that's when it's time to commit to making changes and reviewing the possible impact of discoveries you made answering all my questions. Because businesses that thrive with nurtured environments create their own kind of 'green'—and you can take that to the bank.

Chapter Six:
Keys To Extraordinary Health

Thirty Days to Better Health
Written By Laura Kobus

Years ago, if you referred to someone as "healthy," it usually meant that they ate right and exercised. Today's definition of health consists of much more—it includes emotional and spiritual health as well.

It has been scientifically proven over and over that there is a direct connection between the mind and the body. The word 'disease' really means dis-ease, the exact opposite of ease. Though other factors such as genetics and the aging process can significantly influence our physical health, it can be astonishing when you realize that how we think can determine how we feel. We ponder questions such as "Do we really hold the power for what happens to us physically?" "Are we responsible for causing disease in our bodies?"

My answer is a resounding "yes." Louise Hay, author of "You Can Heal Your Life," seems to agree. In fact she believes that we are each 100% responsible for all of our experiences, good or bad. In her book she tells the story of how she healed herself from cancer through changing the mental patterns that she felt created disease. Here are some of her points:

- We create every so-called "illness" in our body.
- Every thought we think is creating our future.
- The bottom line for everyone is, "I'm not good enough."
- Resentment, criticism and guilt are the most damaging patterns.
- Releasing resentment will even dissolve cancer.
- We must release the past and forgive everyone.
- Self-approval and self-acceptance is the key to positive changes.
- When we really love ourselves, everything in our life works.

The way to better health is to become aware of the factors that compromise your health and take action to re-program your mind, body and spirit to support wellness instead.

By completing the exercises in each category and committing to a thirty day program, you will start feeling more energized, uplifted and enjoying a healthier life.

Step 1: Re-Program Your Mind:

What kind of emotions cause us to become physically ill? Stress, Anxiety, Depression, Worry, Fear, Guilt and Anger to name a few. Instead of allowing these negative emotions to control you, learn to control them.

Here are techniques designed to reduce stress and help you to feel lighter and more energetic. The best part is that they only take a few minutes and you can do them anywhere, anytime without the help of a professional. Choose which ones appeal to you the most and incorporate them into your daily routine.

a) **Deep Breathing**—Most people tend to breathe in short, shallow breaths when under stress. Deep breathing, if practiced daily, will help to reduce anxiety by increasing oxygen, thus calming the mind and increasing energy. Take a deep breath, hold it for 5 seconds, and then breathe out for another 5 seconds. Repeat 5-10 times.

b) **Progressive Muscle Relaxation**—Have you ever noticed just how tense your body is at times? Massages are great, but here is a quick way to relieve tension when you don't have access to one. Starting with your head, tense all the muscles in your face and hold for 5 seconds. Then release quickly. Repeat this process, tensing each muscle group as you work your way down to your feet.

c) **Visualization Techniques**—When you're feeling out of sorts, shift into a higher gear through visualizing what you want in your life. You can also imagine a beautiful scene such as a tropical island. Make the picture as vivid and bright as possible, focusing on your five senses until you actually feel like you're really there.

d) **Positive Thinking**—What you focus on expands. If you find yourself thinking negative thoughts, quickly replace them with positive ones. This will train your brain to start thinking positively on a daily basis.

e) **Live in the Present Moment**—Though it is physically impossible to live in the past or future, many of us still try to. This creates anxiety and robs you of experiencing life fully.

f) **Laughter**—It's still the best medicine. It gets you to lighten up and not take yourself and life so seriously.

g) **Slow Down**—A frantic schedule results in a chaotic mind and tense body. Stop rushing through life and actually live it.

h) **Simplify Your Life**—When your life is simpler, you are calmer. How much "stuff" do you really need anyway? There is a saying "We come into the world with nothing and we leave with nothing." Focus on what's most important and eliminate the rest.

i) **Build a Support System**—Sometimes we are so busy supporting others that we forget we need the same in return. Don't be afraid to reach out to friends or family, and remember, other people like to feel needed too.

j) **Forgive Yourself and Others**—This is the quickest way to releasing anger and achieving inner peace.

k) **Feel the Fear and Do it Anyway**—Take the risks that you've been avoiding and watch how good you'll feel. Believe it or not, it's actually easier to push through fear than to avoid it. Avoidance simply makes fear multiply.

Action Step:

Choose one of the previous strategies for the first week, list it at week 1 and practice it daily. For week 2, add a second strategy. Follow this process for weeks 3 and 4 and by the end of the month you will have 4 new strategies to get you on track to feeling great!

Week 1:

Week 2:

Week 3:

Week 4:

Step #2: Re-Program Your Body:

Your body is similar to a car in that if you clean it, care for it and feed it high test fuel, it will run smoothly and last a lot longer. The first thing I recommend is to get a physical that includes a blood workup to rule out any potential problems. Next, review the following, which is essential to keeping your body in good shape:

a) **A Healthy Diet**—To feel good, eat healthy foods that you enjoy but avoid overeating. If you want to learn more about healthy foods, pick up a book or visit a nutritionist. For weight loss, I don't recommend any specific diets. For many people dieting does not work. If you find yourself overeating, it's usually due to emotional reasons, not because you are still hungry. The acronym HALT stands for Hungry, Angry, Lonely, Tired. Next time you're tempted to overeat or consume rich, calorie-loaded foods, HALT and ask yourself "what am I really feeling and what do I want instead?" You may realize that calling a friend or taking a nap would support your needs much more than eating would. Listen to your body for signals as to what, when, and how much to eat. It knows what's best for you. Keeping a food diary may be helpful also. Design an eating plan that works for you. List 4 habits (one for each week) you can implement to support you. For example, one week you may want to shift from sugar to natural sweeteners or no sweeteners. The next, replace white flour with whole wheat flour.

b) **Good Personal Grooming**—Take pride in your appearance by taking good care of your skin, hair and nails and body. Wear colors and styles that enhance you, rather than detract from you. When you look good, you'll feel good. Each day, take two minutes to focus on a different part of your body. One day you may decide to use a facial mask or scrub, the next day focus on your nails, etc.

c) **Rest & Relaxation**—Get enough sleep so that you will have plenty of energy throughout the day. The amount of sleep required is different for everyone. Plan a fun or relaxing activity that you look forward to when you're not working. Treat yourself to a massage. It not only feels great and helps relax tense muscles but increases circulation as well.

d) **Regular Exercise**—Strive for at least 3 times per week for a minimum of thirty minutes. Do what you enjoy most. There are so many types of exercise that you can do even if you have physical limitations. A few suggestions are swimming, bike-riding, aerobics, running, walking, dancing, team sports or horseback riding.

Action Step:

Choose a specific item from each category and implement it daily for that week. List what you will do. Add something new each week.

Week 1 (Diet):

Week 2 (Grooming):

Week 3 (R&R):

Week 4 (Exercise):

Step #3: Re-Program Your Spirit:

Nurture your soul by engaging in activities to connect with your inner wisdom. The following suggestions can guide you in this direction.

a) **Prayer**—When praying for yourself or someone else, don't forget to give thanks as well for all of your blessings.

b) **Place of Worship**—Surrounding yourself with like-minded people provides a great sense of connection and support.

c) **Meditation**—There is no right or wrong way to meditate. You may want to close your eyes or light a candle, but the important thing is to just let your body and mind be still and quiet.

d) **Walking in Nature**—This is very relaxing and a meditation in itself. Focusing on all five senses will further enhance your experience.

e) **Journaling**—A great way to empty your mind is by putting your thoughts on paper. Enjoy the insights!

f) **Quiet Time Alone**—Remove yourself from the busyness of everyday life and get clear on what's most important by reflecting inward.

Action Step:

Choose one activity and implement it daily for that week. List what you will do. Add a new activity each week.

Week 1:

Week 2:

Week 3:

Week 4:

At the end of your thirty day program, notice what changed and what results you received. What actions did you take that proved most significant in improving your health in each category?

Mind—Results:

What worked best?

Body—Results:

What worked best?

Spirit—Results:

What worked best?

Congratulations! By creating your personal thirty day wellness program, you've just taken a huge step towards feeling the best that you can in mind, body and spirit. I hope you're enjoying the results that *you* have created. I wish you a long, happy and healthy life.

Chapter Seven:
The Power of Your Time

Fourteen Steps To Managing Your Time Effectively
Written By Laura Kobus

I wish I had more time.

How often have you said that to yourself? Probably as often as thousands of others who struggle with the concept of time management. Rest assured, though, that you are not alone. I have also experienced the frustration of feeling as if there was never enough time to get things done. I was habitually late for appointments, and undertaking projects seemed so overwhelming that I would procrastinate until the last minute, just sliding in under the deadline. I saw time as a something elusive, always just beyond my grasp, and was mystified by those who seemed to be successful at managing their time and accomplishing their goals. To say my world was stressful and out of control was an understatement—until the day I made the decision to take back my life.

Determined to conquer the chaos, I prepared myself for the task. The first step was realizing that I had the power to change myself and my life. I decided to look at time as my friend instead of my enemy. This involved studying people who were effective time managers and learning their secrets. I took seminars and read books on the subject. I also went through a self-assessment process where I had to be totally honest with myself to identify what kept me "stuck."

I've learned that I feel positive to the degree that I am in control of my life. Conversely, I feel negative to the degree that I am *not* in control of my life. In the pages that follow, I will share with you fourteen steps that will help you to reclaim your power and take control of *your* life.

1. **Practice Mindfulness.** Spend some quiet time each day in reflection journaling, meditation, or walking in nature. This enables you to relax, be in the moment and brings your attention to what's most important. Never let the urgent crowd out the important. We all have tasks that are urgent and need to be attended to before the day's end, but beware of getting so caught up in the frenzy of putting out fires that you neglect the things that you really value and keep you centered, such as spending quality time alone or with a family member.

2. **Evaluate How You Are Spending Your Time vs. How You Really Want To Spend Your Time.**

   The following exercise will help illustrate this as well as determine if your life is in balance:

   a. Take a blank sheet of paper and draw a line across the page, separating it into two sections. In the top section, draw a circle and make a pie chart (like a pizza pie, only, with nine slices). Cut the slices in the appropriate width and label them according to how you are currently spending your time. Listed are some categories to guide you. You may use one category for each section, combine some of them, or substitute your own categories.

   1) Finances
   2) Health & Fitness
   3) Relationship
   4) Family
   5) Friends
   6) Personal/Spiritual Growth
   7) Rest/Relaxation/Fun
   8) Home Environment
   9) Profession

   b. Rate the level of importance of each category in your life (1-9) by writing the number in that particular slice of pie. If you have a tie, write the same number twice.

   c. Now draw another circle below the line. Then draw the slices again according to how you *really* want to spend your time.

Contemplative Questions:

What does this exercise tell you about how you spend your time vs. how you really want to spend your time?

What actions could you take so that your life would more closely resemble the second circle?

3. **Determine Your Long And Short Term Goals.** When your goals are clear, your energy is channeled in a specific direction, therefore, the time you spend working toward achieving them will be more focused and productive than if you haven't set any goals. To get started, ask yourself: "What do I value most in life?" Picture your future 3-5 years from now. Work back from there to the present. Create goals with a specific time-line. I recommend that you create a detailed vision of what you want along with yearly plan which you can break down into four quarters. Then create action steps for each goal. Goals are much more likely to be achieved if there is a daily or weekly action step attached to them. An example of this process is illustrated.

    A client of mine wanted to buy her first home. She saw herself living in her ideal home by the summer of 2007 (three years from now). She pictured everything that she wanted in her ideal home including the style, color, layout, furnishings…even the neighborhood. She needed to have at least $30,000.00 saved for a down payment. Her yearly goal was to save $10,000.00 each year for the next three years. In order to do that, a savings of 2,500.00 every quarter was required, which amounted to approximately $830 per month.

    Her action steps for the first four weeks were as follows:

    <u>Week One</u>—Develop a budget that would require her to save approximately $200 per week.
    <u>Week Two</u>—Set up a direct deposit account with automatic paycheck deductions of $50 per week.

Week Three—Cut down on food expenses by bringing lunch to work and eating out only once per week.

Week Four—Review investment accounts with advisor and make any recommended changes.

By setting goals and committing to weekly action steps, she is managing her time in an effective way designed to produce the results she wants. Not only is she saving $200 per week but the dream of owning her own home is now turning into reality.

Contemplative Questions:

Check in with yourself periodically to see if you are on track to reach your goals by asking yourself the following:

What am I trying to accomplish?

Is what I'm doing now leading to my ideal future?

How am I trying to do it?

What is going well?

What do I need to change?

4. **Make Detailed Plans.** Since action without planning is not always productive, I encourage you to set yourself up for success by planning on a continuous basis. Get into the habit of thinking on paper as things become clearer when you do this. Review your plans regularly and make

necessary changes. Planning makes you on a more efficient time manager, because if you are clear on what needs to be done, you can schedule a specific date and time frame to complete those tasks.

5. **Use A Time Management System.** Whether an electronic or paper planner, it's crucial to have a time management system that works for you one a daily basis. I found this out the hard way, having used a wall calendar and writing my appointments in the boxes. As my schedule got busier, you can imagine the stress I encountered when I missed appointments because I didn't have the calendar in front of me at all times! If you are a visual person and like to flip pages to see previous and upcoming weeks, then a paper planner is best. I have one from "At a Glance," which I love because it is large (8-1/2 x 11) and broken into 15 minute time increments throughout the day, allowing you to see the entire week at a glance. The disadvantages are that if you lose the planner, you're in trouble, or if other people need access to your calendar, it is hard to share it with them.

    Also, if you are more of a linear/digital person, have recurring appointments, and are a heavy computer user, you may prefer a computerized calendar or portable electronic planner, known as a personal digital assistant (PDA). Having both is optimal as you can synchronize your computer calendar with your palm pilot. But, no matter what system you choose, just choose one. Making the commitment is more important than the specific format you choose.

6. **Create A Weekly And Daily To-Do List.** To start off the week ahead on a good note, create a weekly to-do list on Sunday. Then take items from your list and schedule them into your planner in a specific time slot. The act of transferring items directly to your planner will be a stronger guarantee that they will get done. A good rule of thumb is not to do anything that's not on the list unless it's an emergency.

7. **Prioritize, Delegate, Eliminate.** It's helpful when prioritizing to ask yourself the following questions:

    What is the most valuable use of my time right now? What tasks are vital and urgent?

    What am I really good at and if done well, will make a big difference in my life or career?

We get a feeling of energy and confidence when it contributes to achieving major goals.

Remember the 80-20 rule. 20% of what you do will account for 80% of your results. A good way to prioritize projects is the ABCDE method:

A = Urgent. Must be done today to avoid negative consequences.
B = Important but not crucial. Can be done within a few days.
C = Can be done by the end of the week.
D = Delegate (Delegate as much as you can—especially things you don't like doing)
E = Eliminate

If you prefer using numbers instead of letters, that will work as well. The important thing is to have some kind of system or else there is no way to distinguish one project from the next. Avoiding confusion helps you to avoid feeling overwhelmed.

8. **Expedite Reading Material.** Take a course in speed-reading. With regard to magazines and books, look at the table of contents and highlight the articles or chapters you want to read. For books, highlight the chapters that look the most interesting and read them first. For articles, tear them out of the magazine (a box cutter works great) and make a "to read" file. Keep the file either at home or in your car so you can read during down time, then throw the magazines away. Regarding subscriptions, only keep what you really love and cancel the rest. You can get most of them online, anyway.

9. **Don't Double Handle Papers.** This is a common mistake many people make. When you have a paper in your hand, decide whether you will act on it, file it, or trash it.

10. **Organize Your Home And Office.** An organized living and work space promotes a clear mind. You will also be able to find things more easily.

11. **Control Interruptions.** Hold phone calls or let the answering machine take them when working on something important, and then return them all at the same time. Batch other tasks as well, including correspondence, e-mails, etc.

12. **Put An End To Chronic Lateness.** There are some times when lateness is unavoidable due to circumstances beyond our control. Chronic lateness, however, can only result in negative outcomes such as missed opportunities, stress, anger, lowered self-esteem and even accidents. I don't believe that chronically late people ever intend to be rude to others—they are simply caught up in their own turmoil. Even though you may have the best intentions, lateness is perceived by others as a lack of respect for their time. And we all know how valuable time is! One of the most common reasons for lateness is trying to do too much in too little time. It's like the popular saying "You can't stuff ten pounds of baloney into a five pound bag." How many of you say to yourself on a consistent basis: "I have time to fit in just one more thing before I leave." If this sounds familiar, the key here is to be *really* honest with yourself.

I was a pro at this. I could actually trick my mind into believing I could do that one last thing. When I found myself late, however, the frustration and anxiety that resulted was far worse than not being able to get everything done. To be on time, evaluate how much time everything takes and allow 15-20 minutes extra. Another suggestion is to indicate the time in your planner you need to leave for an appointment as well as the actual appointment time. You can also try setting an alarm for five minutes before the time you have to leave. This can be in the form of a cell phone, pager, kitchen timer, or clock alarm. When you master the art of being on time, you will most likely find the rewards of being relaxed, centered, and productive so great that you may wonder why it took so long.

Contemplative Question:

What do I have to do to be on time?

13. **Stop Procrastinating.** I've found procrastinating to be one of the most common habits among those who are "time challenged." Listed are the eight main reasons behind procrastination and some solutions you can implement to put an end to this self-destructive habit.

Reason #1:   The task is unpleasant.

Solution: *Either get it over with promptly or find someone else to do it.* Make a list of the benefits of getting it done. This will help create momentum.

Reason #2:   The task is unplanned and the goal is not clear.

Solution: *Ask yourself what information you need to begin.* What is the game plan? Example: If the task is to design your ideal office, break it down further into sub-categories and ask yourself questions such as, "What design, color scheme, lighting, etc. do I want?"

Reason #3:   The task seems overwhelming.

Solution: *Accomplish it by "chunking it down."* Develop blocks of time to work on the task by breaking the job into bite size pieces. In a recent workshop I gave on time management, I found a creative and effective way to illustrate this analogy by passing out Nestle Chunky Bars to the participants! They all got a big kick out of it. Handling just one part of a project makes it easier to actually start it. You may gain momentum & want to do more, but at least you'll have started. It's also best not to combine functional and creative tasks. Creative tasks take a minimum of 60–90 minutes of unbroken time. The best time is in the morning when you are fresh, but if you are a night person, by all means do it at night.

I remember the feeling of "overwhelm" when I first started writing resumes. Because it is a creative process and took a few hours, I would put it off because I didn't seem to have a block of time that large at one sitting. Then I would cram the night before the resume was due, causing myself undue stress. The most difficult part of a resume is determining the layout (chronological, functional or combination) and writing the profile or summary of qualifications. When I chose to block out an hour or so for that, the rest flowed with ease.

Reason #4:   **You fear failure.**
Solution: *Feel the fear and do it anyway.*
First of all, there is no such thing as failure—everything is a learning experience. Here is a golden nugget: *Pushing through fear is actually easier than avoiding it.* If you wait for the fear to dissipate before doing something, you may wait forever. You then become stuck in inertia, hence the expression "paralyzed with fear." It becomes a snowball effect, since the longer you put something off, the scarier it becomes. Since it's not always possible to be certain of the outcome beforehand, taking action despite your fear will build momentum and confidence. Once you're involved, you can then evaluate the situation and make changes if necessary. The process of involvement usually causes fear to subside. If you are still procrastinating at this point, realize that the pain of not taking action is very often worse than taking action and risking mistakes.

Reason #5:   **You over commit.**
Solution: *Review your life and the results of the pie chart exercise on how you spend your time.*
Let go of any extraneous commitments. Practice saying "no" to others, and be extremely careful about any future commitments.

Reason #6:   **You're addicted to drama and chaos.**
Solution: *Make the decision to jump off the merry-go-round.*
There are people who seek drama to avoid looking at reality. They see life without drama as boring. This is a sign that they need to slow down and redefine their life. If this sounds like you, focus on the benefits of being more relaxed. Practice being in the present moment. Spend some time alone with the most important person in your life—yourself.

Reason #7:   **You're a perfectionist.**
Solution: *Give yourself a deadline and stick to it.*
You might also schedule a task right after that to avoid going overtime. To put a project into perspective, ask

yourself, "How much difference will it really make if I spend a little more time on this?" If there was no deadline for this article, it may have very well turned into an entire book! Also realize that perfectionism and fear of failure go hand in hand.

Reason #8   You're indecisive.
Solution: *Realize there is no perfect decision.*
                  Most of the time one decision is not a lot better than another. Remember the equation: over analysis = paralysis. I love the quote by Eric Carle: "You can't plow a field by turning it over in your mind." Another technique to try is relating the choices to your priorities and then letting your intuition or "gut feeling" take over.

                  Contemplative Questions:

                  What is procrastinating costing me?

                  What am I committed to doing about it?

14. **Practice Time Awareness Exercises.** Complete the following phrases with as many responses as you can:

I know I'm too busy when:

I will make time for:

List three ways that you waste your time (examples: excessive e-mail or voice mail checking, T.V. watching, long phone conversations, worrying, searching for your keys).

1.
2.
3.

Next, write three action steps that you could take to stop these behaviors.

1.
2.
3.

List three areas of your life where you can save time.

1.
2.
3.

Now, write three action steps you can take.

1.
2.
3.

Even rock and roll singers agree that time is a precious commodity. Here are three verses from popular songs written about time.

- *Life is so brief and time is a thief when you're undecided. And like a fistful of sand it can slip right through your hands.* **Rod Stewart**
- *Time waits for no one.* **The Rolling Stones**
- *Ticking away the moments that make up a dull day. You fritter and waste the hours in an offhand way.* **Pink Floyd**

The good news is that anyone can develop the skill of effective time management. Once you've realized the value of it and how it can change your life, the next step is to put what you've learned into action on a daily basis. All it takes is desire, determination and commitment. After all, isn't it worth your time?

Conclusion

Once upon a time, a person roaming across a countryside fell down an abandoned well. Unhurt, he tried to grasp the sides of the well to climb out. But it was dark and the surface didn't seem to have any spots for him to grab a hold. "Help! Help!" he cried. After some time, a friend, a fellow wanderer, heard him and peered down into the well. "What's happened?" he called down. "I can't get out!" cried his friend. "Please—go for help! I'm scared!" With that, his friend leapt down into the well with him. "Why did you do that?" said the man in frustration. "Now we're both stuck down here!" "That's true, friend" said the other. "But I've been here before and I know the way out."

The moral of the story? Whatever in your life you are not happy with, someone is available to share the experience and help you. Be willing to reach out, ask for help and you'll find the support you need.

In these chapters you've been exposed to a variety of techniques to help you design a winning life. It does not matter how you define that life as long as it feels natural for you and it provides the opportunity for ongoing growth and success in any endeavor you undertake or any challenge you face.

And, despite the variety of authors, the topics and the personal styles you've read, we all have one very important feature in common—the sincere wish for you to feel a sense of encouragement as you undergo changes and our complete support for you to make these changes. As coaches we know that change is both difficult and inevitable. It's invaluable to have a resource you can turn to that applauds your willingness to face change, head on, to keep you on the path you've set and, where appropriate, help you discover and define just what that path is. We hope this book has been that resource for you.

If you think you may have found someone in these pages who really gets you, please turn to our Author Bio's section at the end of this book to locate your coach.

And, if you'd like to find out more about coaching and whether this profession may be for you, please visit our web site http://www.unitedcoachingassociates.com You can also e-mail us at uca@unitedcoachingassociates.com

Good luck to you!

Author Bio's (Who We Are):

Andrea Feinberg, Small Business and Marketing Coach

I have been self-employed, as consultant and coach, for 16 years. I've worked with clients in a broad variety of industries including the investment markets, publishing, banking, health & beauty aids, wholesale gift, medical, retail, software/hardware sales, handcrafts. This diversity, including my experiences as corporate employee, small business owner and coach/consultant has expanded my perspective to see business from many sides. When I'm not working, you may find me on stage with Long Island's community theater groups.

Types of Clients I Work With:

Coaching Insight is committed to supporting small, new and soon-to-be business owners in their desire to achieve marketing success, effective time management, visionary leadership, enhanced employee performance.

How is this done? By identifying and maximizing your unique skill set, priorities, resources and hidden assets—in your business, your employees & in yourself.

I absolutely believe you've got the key to success within you, right now.

Do any of these statements sound like you?

- I'm constantly putting out fires and can't take time to plan for the future.
- I need to enhance business productivity but can't work any harder than I am.
- I can't remember why I thought I'd enjoy business ownership
- I need somebody to bounce ideas around, to give me some feedback.
- I want more than just the income; I want to build something lasting.
- I'd like to make more effective decisions but sometimes I'm just brain dead.
- I've got to do everything myself if it's going to get done right.
- This place would fall apart if I took a vacation.
- I'd like to attract and keep productive, creative employees.

- I simply have no time—for family, friends, hobbies, or me.
- Of course I want the business to grow and thrive, I'm just out of ideas right now.
- I'm new at this and want to be sure the leap to business ownership is right for me.
- I'm constantly worried about what should have been done yesterday or what has to get done tomorrow—I'm rarely focused on right now.

What's In It For You:

You have assets that you have not fully utilized—a unique combination of skills and resources from which something fresh and vibrant can be created.

As your business coach, I will ensure that you capitalize on every one of your strengths and abilities.

When you focus on operating from your unique strengths, and not on overcoming weaknesses, the result for you is dramatic:

- Improve the effectiveness of your choices (you work smart, not hard)
- Streamline the cost of doing business (you save money)
- Simplify the choices you make (you get clarity and direction)
- Gain a sense of ease and power in all you do (you get your passion back)
- Lose a huge source of stress (you get your life back)

Education and Professional Background:

- Vice President and Director of Strategic Growth for the United Coaching Associates, Inc.
- New York University, MBA, Marketing
- Coach U, Graduate
- CoachVille, Founding Member
- Board member, Foundation for Sight & Sound
- Adjunct Instructor, Hofstra University
- *Westbury Chamber of Commerce, Past President
- Long Island Wellness Day, Founder & Chair
- Profiled in: Newsday, Long Island Business News, Westbury Times
- Published in: Business to Business, Newsline, The Hauppauge Reporter, Creations Magazine, Scleroderma Journal, LI Women.com

Contact Information:

Andrea Feinberg, Business Coach and Consultant
Company Name: Coaching Insight
Voice: 631-642-7434
E-mail: <u>andreafeinberg@optonline.net</u>
Web-site: <u>www.coachinginsight.com</u>

I Offer A Free Initial 30-Minute Coaching Call.

Bonnie Schizzano, R.N., Inner Fitness Coach

Bonnie Schizzano is a warm, inspiring personal coach, speaker and trainer and the founder and president of Healing Inside Out, a coaching and training organization. She is the developer of a unique coaching approach, which she calls Inner Fitness Transformation, a synthesis of coaching, Neuro-Linguistic Programming, Ericksonian Hypnosis, visualization and holistic nursing.

The types of clients who hire Bonnie as their coach, are experiencing stress, overwhelm, dissatisfaction or have "plateaued" in an important area of their life. Through the process of coaching, clients stop just getting by and learn how to get through to the other side, becoming self-empowered and excited about the possibilities that await them.

Specialty Areas Of Coaching Approach Are:

- Pro-Active Living—Make the Fullest use of your Talents and Resources
- Dissolving Stress & Anxiety—Turn Challenges into Opportunities
- Nurturing the Nurse—Taking care of #1 for a Change
- Beyond & Back—Living Free from Addictions

Bonnie Is The Facilitator Of These Popular Programs:

- Creating Living—Do Less & Live More
- Your Life Matters—Setting Goals & Outcomes
- Pro-Active Procrastination
- Inner Fitness 1 & 2
- Inside Insight's for Motivating Others
- Beyond & Back—Living is Learning
- Mind POWER
- Self-Hypnosis; Hypnosis 1 Certification Training; Meditation & Tele classes

Bonnie Schizzano's certifications include: Life Coach, Master Practitioner of Neuro-Linguistic Programming, Master Hypnotherapist and Trainer, Silva Ultramind System and Reiki Master. She is a founding member of the United Coaching Associates and a member of CoachVille. She is also a licensed Registered Nurse.

Contact Information:

Bonnie Schizzano, Inner Fitness Coach
Telephone: 631-588-3990
Email: healinginsideout@verizon.net
Web-site: www.healinginsideout.com

Give yourself, this wonderful opportunity and experience a 30-minute complimentary coaching session to:

- break through self imposed limitations
- journey inside and get in touch with your strengths and resources
- enhance your relationships for greater intimacy and enjoyment
- create a vision for your future

Crescendo Associates: Patti Bloom, M.S., R.M.T. and Fred Strauss, C.C.P.

Crescendo Associates focuses on assisting individual clients and businesses to "orchestrate their growth through dynamic change." This is affected by strategically identifying the concerns of the client, assessing the current environment, designing and implementing a process to achieve their business and personal goals.

Crescendo Associates conducts in-service training programs tailored to meet the individual needs of our clients. Through coaching and mentoring we assist clients in improving the effectiveness and efficiency of their business processes. We mediate conflict in the workplace, which reduces the cost to the employer, resulting in a more productive organization.

Types of Clients We Work With:

Our target clients are corporate executives and middle managers, financial advisors, educators, and people in transition due to life changing events.

Specialties:

- Individual and Group Coaching
- Consulting
- Training Seminars
- Mediation Systems Design
- Task Analysis
- Mentoring Programs
- Change Management

Other Business and Organization Involvements:

- United Coaching Associates
- CoachVille
- Long Island Association
- Hauppauge Industrial Association
- Long Island Works
- Association of Information Technology Professionals
- Association for Training and Development

- Huntington Chamber of Commerce/Business Partnership
- Long Island Forum for Technology
- Long Island Software and Technology Network—LISTnet
- Mediation Training Institute
- American Music Therapy Association
- Council for Exceptional Children

Education and Professional Background:

Patti Bloom, M.S., R.M.T.

- Master of Science in Special Education, Hunter College, New York
- Bachelor of Science in Music Therapy, City University of New York
- Permanent NYS Teaching Certificate in Special Education
- Registered Music Therapist—American Music Therapy Association
- Member of Council for Exceptional Children
- Member of the School of Coaching
- Private practice in Early Intervention services for multi-handicapped infants and toddlers.
- Principal of private special education school in New York City.
- Special education teacher of multi-handicapped children
- Music therapist for varying populations of handicapped individuals
- Grant writing, budget analysis, in-service training programs
- Speaker's Bureau, public speaking, workshops and seminars

Fred Strauss, C.C.P.

- Post Graduate Studies Polytechnic University,
- Master of Science, Computer Science Polytechnic Institute of New York
- Systems Management, University of Southern California
- Bachelor of Science, EE/Computer Science, Arizona State University
- FJS Associates and Business Information Systems—Founder and President—We Specialize in Systems Engineering (all life cycle phases), Project Management; Mentoring and Coaching; Conflict Resolution and Mediation; Business Process Reengineering; Quality Assessment and Certification; and Training.
- Professor of Computer Science and Management, Polytechnic University
- Director CIS programs, Polytechnic University, Long Island Graduate Center
- Publications in Professional Refereed Journals

- Adjunct and on-line Professor, Syracuse University, Briarcliffe College, NYIT
- School of Coaching
- Certified Trainer, Mediation Training Institute
- Certified Computer Professional
- Arizona Board of Technical Registration (EIT)
- Book Editor, SIGS Publications, McGraw Hill, Prentice Hall
- Magazine Editor for the X-Journal and UNIX Developer

Awards:

Patti Bloom:

- Numerous professional workshops and presentations
- Television appearances—CBS and NBC News

Fred Strauss:

- Award of Excellence—National Center for Disability Services
- Outstanding Faculty Member—Dowling College
- AT&T Outstanding Sales Award
- AT&T Silver Sales Award for Outstanding Sales
- New York State Medal for Conspicuous Service

Contact Information:

Crescendo Associates
PO Box 1455
Melville NY 11747

Patti Bloom, M.S., R.M.T.
Voice: 631-786-9222
CrescendoAssoc@aol.com

Fred Strauss, C.C.P.
Voice: 631-921-1055
CrescendoAssoc@yahoo.com

We offer a complimentary consultation.

Deborah Brown-Volkman, Career and Mentor Coach

I am the President of *Surpass Your Dreams, Inc.*, a successful career and mentor coaching company that has been delivering a message of motivation, success, and personal fulfillment since 1998. We work with Senior Executives, Vice Presidents, and Managers who are out of work or overworked. We also work with Coaches who want to start and build successful coaching practices. Our clients are those who want to hear something different so they can make something different happen in their careers.

Current and former clients include individuals from: *JPMorganChase, Oracle Corporation, Lucent Technologies, General Motors, Procter & Gamble, Ziff Davis, IBM, American Express, EDS, Ogilvy & Mather, McCann-Erickson Worldgroup, Columbia University, New York University, Chief Executive Magazine, MSNBC, & BMW.*

I am a Published Writer and my articles on how to be successful in your career can be found on more than 100 web-sites over the Internet. I am the Author of two books titled *Coach Yourself To A New Career: A Guide For Discovering Your Ultimate Profession*, and *Four Steps To Building A Profitable Coaching Practice: A Complete Marketing Resource Book For Coaches*. I also write a e-mail newsletter and weekly tips titled: Surpass Your Dreams that offers you practical advice and steps so Monday can be the best day of your week.

I have been featured as a career expert for WABC-TV New York Eyewitness News, CNN, News 12, The Wall Street Journal, The New York Times, Smart Money Magazine, The Chicago Tribune, and New York Newsday. I was also a featured guest on BBC, Radio Scotland when they came to New York City to find out how people were coping in their careers since the September 11th attacks.

Specialties:

Career Change, Career Development, Career Effectiveness, and Mentor Coaching

Types of Clients I Work With:

Coaches, CEO's, Financial Service Executives, Internet Executives, Marketing Executives, Managers, Vice-Presidents, and Senior Executives.

Education and Background:

- President and Founder of the United Coaching Associates, Inc.
- Graduate of Coach University's Accredited Coaches Training Program in Business and Personal Coaching
- Enrolled in CoachVille's Graduate School of Coaching
- Founding Member of Coachville.com
- Charter Member of the ICF-New York City Speakers Bureau
- Member of the International Coach Federation
- Member of the Long Island Association
- Member of the Hauppauge Industrial Association
- LongIsland.com Career Expert
- BA in Marketing from Hofstra University
- AAS degree in Data Processing from Queensborough Community College
- Certificate in Financial Planning from New York University
- 12 Years Experience Running Sales & Marketing Programs for Fortune 500 companies and dot.coms

Professional Background:

Financial Services, The Internet, Marketing, Sales, and Web Technology

Contact Information:

Contact: Deborah Brown-Volkman, President, Surpass Your Dreams, Inc.
President & Founder, United Coaching Associates, Inc.
Telephone Number: 631-874-2877
E-mail: info@surpassyourdreams.com
Web-site: www.surpassyourdreams.com

I Offer A Free Initial 30-Minute Get Acquainted & Goal-Setting Coaching Call.

Donna M. Krebs, M.B.A., Personal Development Coach

I am the bandleader of InnerImage, Unlimited, a coaching practice dedicated to working with individuals who want to take stretching steps forward in their life with focus, direction and purpose. I partner with a client to create and execute a plan that will deliver what they want most out of life, personal freedom and confidence to achieve their dreams and goals.

Born and raised in New York, I am living happily with my husband of 17 years with our two growing boys and Cairn terrier on Long Island. I'm a 2002 graduate of Coach U's Coach Training Program which is the largest coach training program accredited by the International Coach Federation (ICF). I've also achieved a certification in Toltec Wisdom Coaching from Ray Dodd, a Master Belief Coach and apprentice of Don Miguel Ruiz, best-selling author of the 'The Four Agreements.' Last, but not least, I'm a certified professional Information Technology Project Manager.

Education:

- Bachelor of Professional Studies degree in Computer Science, L.I.U— C.W. Post
- M.B.A. degree in Finance, L.I.U.—C.W. Post

Memberships:

- Charter member of the United Coaching Association (UCA)
- Member of CoachVille's School of Personal Development
- Member of the International Association of Coaches (IAC)
- Member of the Project Management Institute (PMI)

Contact Information:

Donna M. Krebs, Personal Development Coach
InnerImage, Unlimited
Email: InnerImageU@hotmail.com
Office #: 516-543-3911

Note: Give yourself permission to explore new horizons in happiness and personal growth. I welcome the opportunity to get acquainted with you to determine if we're a good fit for one another and if I can assist you in reaching your inner 'personal best'. Your very first 60-minute call with me is my gift to you.

Grace E. McAliece, Career Coach

Coaching Statement: As a Career Coach I help my young clients get crystal clear about their ideal career path. I want my clients to identify and create the career of their dreams. My clients are guided by their own awareness and choices. I provide the tools for on-going support.

Clients I Love to Coach:

- Those who feel trapped or stuck
- Those needing support for major life choices
- Those looking for their perfect career path
- Those not sure who is making the decisions
- Those feeling like they have done all the right things and they are still unhappy

Coaching Specialties:

- Visualizations
- I am Guiding, Inspiring and in awe of my clients
- Providing a safe environment
- Active listener
- Individual and group sessions

Education and Background:

- Choral award/Regional Choir/Madrigal Group/musicals
- Graduate of COACH FOR LIFE Coach Training Program
- Certificate of Programming
- On-going continued coaching education through coaching organizations and teleclasses
- Director of Membership of the United Coaching Associates

Professional Background:

- President of a computer service organization
- Accounts Receivable manager
- Assisting small business' from accounting, brochure layout to software set-up

- I am self taught in MS Office and most accounting programs
- Extensive experience in training others

Contact Information:

Grace E. McAliece, Career Coach
Lifegem
Phone: 201.805.5379
Email: Lifegem_1@hotmail.com
Web Site: www.lifegem.biz

I Offer A Free 45 minute sample Coaching Call.

Kay Dinehart, Personal, Professional, Spiritual Coach

I believe that each of us come into this world with a unique gift to share which is our life purpose. It is my vision that each of us identifies our purpose and brings it forward in our lives to create the excitement and joy we were meant to experience.

I truly value every person and hold the vision that each will realize their full potential and fulfill their destiny. Working to move others forward has always been one of my greatest values and I have spent my life doing this though my professional and personal life. I raised four wonderful children and as a teacher of children for 25 years enjoyed motivating them to work through their strengths thereby minimizing their weaknesses.

I bring this experience forward in my coaching practice and encourage my clients to dream their grandest vision. We work together in strategizing steps toward attainable goals that will propel them forward. As progress is attained, confidence and excitement build toward weaving purpose and passion into their lives.

Coaching Specialties:

- Personal coaching
- Creating a grand vision which is both exciting and inspiring
- Acknowledging feelings and learning how to discern this information
- Tapping into your wisdom through visualization
- Discovering your purpose and passion
- Life Balance
- Identifying blocks that inhibit growth and stifle energy flow
- Identifying needs and minimizing energy drains
- Identifying values and working through them

Clients:

My clients:

- Trust their wisdom and expand possibilities,
- Challenge their belief systems and choose to create a new reality,
- Choose to take responsibility for their lives,

- Understand their power and use it to move them forward,
- Love the journey as much as the destination,
- Choose to live their dream,
- Recognize their strengths and choose to work through them,
- Choose to create a life of purpose and passion,
- Choose a life rather than a lifestyle,
- Seek balance and spiritual fulfillment,
- Build strategies and take action steps toward their goals,
- Plan a vision and reach it.

Professional Background:

- BA
- MS
- 25 Years Teaching Background
- Coach University Graduate
- United Coaching Associates
- CoachVille

Contact Information:

Kay Dinehart
Freespirit Coaching
631-673-0562
E-mail: coachkay@optonline.net

I offer a complimentary coaching call to see if we are a fit to work together.

Laura Kobus, Personal and Career Coach

I coach people to have a life they love and have more love in their life.

Through coaching with me, my clients are able to reduce their stress, improve their self-image, achieve excellent health and have fulfilling relationships. I also show them how to carve out time for the things that matter most in their lives.

I assist people to discover their ideal career or become more successful at their existing one by identifying their unique talents, passions, values and life purpose. I also prepare effective resumes that will get them an interview at the job of their dreams.

I offer my clients the "**CLEAR** Insight Program"

C—**Clarity**—Get crystal clear on what you really want.
L—**Leverage** your strengths and skills and **learn** what motivates you.
E—**Evaluate** the best method to get what you want with **ease**.
A—**Action**—Develop an action plan.
R—**Results**—Enjoy reaching your goals!

Specialty Areas:

Personal Coaching, Career Coaching, Resume and Cover Letter Development, Interview Preparation, Presentation Skills.

Presentations, Teleclasses and Workshops:

I present on a variety of topics including: "Happiness is a Choice," "Eight Steps to a Great Life," "Find Your Perfect Partner," "The Power of Time Management" and "Discover Your Ideal Career."

Who My Clients Are:

Passionate individuals who value personal growth and development, and who have the desire and willingness to commit to discovering who they are, what they want and taking action to achieve it. My clients include, entrepreneurs, creative types, small business owners, managers, homemakers, new graduates, and those in career transition or interested in improving their existing careers.

What We Can Work On Together:

- How to leverage your strengths and talents in order to find work you love.
- How to align your work and life with your principles and priorities.
- How to create and maintain strong relationships that are opportunities for self-expression, integrity and commitment.
- How to restructure your life to have more time, energy and fun.
- How to raise your standards, attract better opportunities and increase your income.
- How to achieve and maintain excellent health and fitness.
- How to increase your level of self-esteem and confidence.
- How to free your mind of limiting beliefs and set yourself up to succeed.

Professional & Educational Background:

- Graduate, Coach For Life Professional Coach Training Program
- CoachVille Graduate School of Coaching Program
- Graduate, Dale Carnegie "Effective Speaking and Human Relations" Program
- Member, United Coaching Associates
- Member, CoachVille

Contact Information:

Clear Insight
Laura Kobus, Personal & Career Coach
Telephone: (631) 427-5566
Fax: (631) 427-5577
E-mail: coaching@optonline.net
Website: www.clearinsightcoaching.com

Discover The 8 Secrets To A Great Life In A Free Introductory Coaching Session.

Leslie K. Malin, MSW, ACSW, Career, Business, and Success Coach

Leslie K. Malin, M.S.W. has enjoyed a successful career as a coach, consultant, speaker, entrepreneur, and psychotherapist for over twenty five years. She founded Management by Design, a company dedicated to evolving business, evolving careers and evolving lives over seventeen years ago. She has trained, coached and consulted with literally thousands of people across industries and inspired them with her vision of what is possible for them in their lives, career and businesses.

Leslie Works With:

Leslie works with successful professionals, executives and entrepreneurs who are feeling overextended, consumed by their work and dispirited and want to reconnect to the creativity, joy and excitement that made them successful; and with business owners who want to craft a new vision and evolve their businesses to the next level.

She has conducted a number of management team coaching initiatives to identify individual strengths and areas of improvement, improve communication and interpersonal relationships and identify areas ripe with untapped opportunity.

She has been a senior outplacement consultant with Manchester Partners, providing career transition coaching to management and senior executives across industries, assisting them in finding new positions, becoming entrepreneurs or moving towards successful, enriching retirement.

Her staff and management retreats never fail to gain raves as she infuses them with exciting interactive experiences, deep personal learning, creative exercises; as well as personal insights that she has gained throughout her own journey in life and career.

Leslie Leads Workshops In:

Leslie is a highly experienced workshop facilitator, having designed and led hundreds of training programs for staff and management personnel in small businesses, large corporations and non-profit organizations.

She is currently very excited about using tele-experiences as a way to reach limitless numbers of people throughout the world who are hungering to learn, develop themselves, connect with like-minded adult learners unimpeded, by distances and cost; while also deepening spiritually. "Tele-classes, using the technology of Bridge Lines, allows the sharing of "bite sized" information that is the preferred method of learning for adults. The classes are learner-driven and as individual as the composition of each participant makes them," says Malin.

Public Speaking and Writing:

Leslie has frequently spoken before conferences, business groups and professional associations such as Lance Secretan's Higher Ground Community, Long Island Business and Professional Women, American Society of Training and Development and Women in Toys, on topics related to work and spirit. She has also been a contributor to articles in Newsday and other publications.

Other Business Involvements:

More recently, Leslie has fulfilled a longstanding dream and has co-created Earth Medicine (www.earth-medicine.com), a business-to-business greeting card company and Estickies (www.estickies.com), a unique e-greetings site that puts your logo in each e-communication. Both sites offer a new voice and look to enhance business-to-business communication with customers, prospects, employees, and colleagues.

Education:

Leslie is a graduate of Vassar College and the Adelphi University School of Social Work, as well as a founding member of CoachVille. Leslie is a life-long learner and has studied with a wide variety of teachers in many disciplines such as Natalie Goldberg, Julia Cameron, Angeles Arrien, Rick Jarow, Gail Straub and many others.

Contact Information:

Leslie Malin, Management by Design
21 Selina Court, Glen Cove, NY 11542
Phone#: 516-671-5662
Fax: 516-671-3493
Email: results@lesliemalin.com
Web site: www.lesliemalincoach.com

Complimentary Decision-Making Coaching Session. As a way for individuals to make an informed decision about whether coaching is right for them, as well as if she is the right "match" and coach for their needs, Leslie offers a complimentary 45 minute coaching session.

Lisa Jaworowski, M.S.W., Personal Development and Career Coach

Why would a licensed psychotherapist with a successful private therapy practice want to be a life coach?

There are many reasons that led me to this choice, but here are two that are especially important to me:

1. I believe that everyone can benefit from having a personal life coach, not just those with a "diagnostic label."

2. Coaching is a highly focused process that brings clients beyond traditional therapy and provides the opportunity to create positive, lasting changes in your life.

My professional background as a Certified Social Worker has included training and experience with individuals and families ranging in age from pre-school children to senior citizens (my oldest client was 100!) It encompasses all stages of life transitions!

Therefore, the skills and techniques I use in coaching have not been just been learned from books or coaching classes; although I continue to use both to enrich my abilities. I am currently receiving Professional Coach Training from CoachVille.

The knowledge and experience I have acquired over the years is based primarily on real life situations and what really "works" for clients who have a strong desire to improve their lives.

Coaching Specialties:

Personal Development-

- Create greater balance between work, family and personal life
- Improve Self Care, Reduce energy drains
- Move forward through lifestyle and career transition periods
- Remain focused and stay motivated towards achieving goals

Career Development

- Pursue Your Dreams
- Identify Career Possibilities
- Resume Development
- Job Search/Interview Skills

Types of Clients I Work With:

Individuals who are ready to put themselves first and create something new and fulfilling for themselves.

- Men and women in lifestyle transitions
- Professionals seeking career changes
- Stay at home" mothers returning to work
- Recent College Graduates
- Overburdened Caregivers

Educational & Professional Background:

- M.S.W., Master of Social Work, Adelphi University, NY
- B.S., Bachelor of Science, Cornell University, NY
- Licensed Clinical Social Worker, New York State (CSW certification)
- Member of NASW Academy of Certified Social Workers (ACSW)
- Member, United Coaching Associates
- Member, CoachVille
- Member, IAC, International Association of Coaches
- Teaching License for "Extreme Self-Care" Program
- Teaching License for "Personal Foundation" Program

Contact Information:

Lisa Jaworowski, Personal Development & Career Coach
Phone (631) 979-4654
Email : LeeJ979@aol.com
Website : www.lisaja.com

I offer a FREE initial 1-hour coaching call.

Lynn B. Engeholm, Life Coach for Women

My mission is to coach women who want to continue their growth in the areas of business, personal fulfillment, and most importantly achieving the harmony within.

I can support you in developing a strategy to get from where you are currently to where you want to be. I am dedicated to our partnership of creating the life you value, by reuniting you with your life's purpose, passion, and power.

I am skilled in supporting women to:

- Change and build careers and businesses;
- Learn how to problem solve;
- Respond to conflict;
- Handle stress;
- Formulate strategies for creating positive relationships;
- Manage their time, money, and physical environment; and
- Discover and utilize their special gifts.

Coaching Specialties:

- Supporting women during organizational instability to find their center of gravity.
- Supporting women develop job search & interview skills based on my perspective as a "hirer."
- Supporting women focus on building <u>reserves</u> so they can lead a balanced life.
- Supporting women to incorporate the same quality planning skills they used in their corporate lives into their personal lives.
- Supporting women work/see their way through situations that seem impossible.
- Supporting women find the space and time to be involved in philanthropic efforts.

Types of Clients I Work With:

Women who are willing to:

- Express their challenges and dreams,
- Grow personally and professionally,

- Take risks, and
- Celebrate their successes.

Professional Background:

My professional career spans more than 25 years. My background is as a computer programmer, data manager, and manager where my analytical, organizational, and leadership skills played an important part in my ability to achieve personal success and to be able to encourage my staff to do the same.

I enjoy working with Non-profit organizations align with their values and mission, and be leaders in their areas of philanthropy.

I Have:

- Hired personnel
- Evaluated and documented performance based on agreed goals
- Kept my direct reports focused and productive during uncertain times
- Led cross functional teams
- Participated on corporate management teams
- Documented policies and procedures
- Advanced my career to Corporate Director

Since 1999, I have been the President of a family philanthropic foundation with my sister and myself being the only staff.

Education:

I received a B.A. in Mathematics from Lindenwood College in St. Charles, Missouri, and a M.B.A. with a specialization in Management from Pace University in New York, New York. I am currently attending Coach U to receive the Professional Certified Coach certificate through the International Coach Federation.

Contact Information:

Lynn B. Engeholm, Life Coach for Women
Telephone: 516 565 5361
Cell: 516 647 6674
Fax: 516 483 0795

I offer a complimentary coaching call to see if we are a fit to work together.

Maris Tain, Professional Life and Transition Coach

Beyond Vision! is committed to impacting lives by empowering individuals to make the ordinary extraordinary and contributing to create a better world. Making a difference together.

As a successful travel consultant in Los Angeles for over 15 years, Maris spent most of her waking hours helping clients design the vacation adventure of their dreams. Aspiring to make a difference on a grander scale, she is now helping her clients design the life of their dreams.

In addition to being a single Mom to her now 27 year-old daughter, Maris has been actively involved in leadership of an international volunteer organization originating from an exceptional Relationship Weekend, for over seven years. She continues in leadership positions, coaching people like you to successful personal and professional relationships, helping them realize their goals and life dreams…successfully Coaching their vision to reality.

"I am committed to inspire and empower my clients to exceed their expectations and realize their full potential, thereby making a difference in their lives and in the world. My clients actively Create Their Vision, Relish Their Joy and Live Their Dream…. Making Their Vision a Reality."

Coaching Specialties:

- Life Balance and Design
- Personal Effectiveness
- Core Dynamics Coaching
- Transition Coaching
- Relationship Coaching
- Assessment Coaching
- Vision/Purpose Exploration

I Work With Individuals Who:

- Are feeling stifled in relationships, career, and life, and are ready to make small to major life changes…
- Are caught up in a dismal routine or busy-ness of life, learn how to laugh again…

- Are too submerged in the roadmap of their calendars, and want to feel joy and excitement again…
- Are still saying "I'll get it done tomorrow," get it done today.
- Are worn out by doing what they think they should be doing, to create their *own* vision toward living the life of their dreams!
- Are very ready to make their visions and dreams their reality, and MAKE A GOOD LIFE GREAT!

Professional Associations and Background:

- Member, CoachVille and Schools of Coaching
- Member, International Association of Coaches
- Member, International Coach Federation
- Member, United Coaching Associates
- Enrolled and training in CoachVille and Graduate Schools of Coaching
- Experienced Coach Program
- Get Certified Virtual Study Group
- Graduate, Sterling Women's Weekend
- Leadership Training and Leadership positions a Women's International Volunteer Organization
- Professional Travel Consultant for over 15 Years

Contact Information:

Maris Tain, Personal and Transition Coach
Phone: 631-427-1306
Email: marisJOYcoach@optonline.net
Web: www.beyondvisioncoaching.com

I offer a ½ hour complimentary Intro "Let's Get Acquainted" call for more information about this adventure called Coaching.

Paula G. Rosario, Personal and Business Coach

Balance and harmony have always been key values in my life and discovering how to achieve these and contribute to the world has leaded me to coaching. It is my passion to support working mothers on their personal journeys to create balance, grace and successful lives. I am in many ways a snapshot of my clients. I am a coach, mother of two young children and a corporate executive with over 20 years' experience in marketing.

Types of Clients I Work With:

My clients are women who have a desire to:

- make self-care a priority in their lives
- strike a comfortable balance between career and family life
- discover their passions and joys
- feel empowered

Professional Background:

For over 20 years I have been in the marketing field, specifically related to the apparel, retail and manufacturing industry. In addition to the vast expertise I've gained from creating marketing communications and promotion strategies, I also mentor and coach individuals and lead business teams to higher performance. Knowing the in's and out's of a corporate climate and what it takes for a working mother to succeed today is invaluable real-life experience I can offer. In addition to coaching, I give workshops on time management, self-care and personal energy.

Memberships Include:

- Graduate of The Fashion Institute of Technology, Marketing & Communications
- Corporate Coach University—currently enrolled
- CoachVille—member
- International Coach Federation—member
- United Coaching Associates—member
- National Retail Federation—member

- The Fashion Group International—member
- The Promotion Marketing Society—member
- The Retail Marketing Society—member

Contact Information:

Paula G. Rosario, Personal & Business Coach
HarmonyQuestCoaching-for your mind, body, and spirit
Paula@harmonyquestcoaching.com
Phone: 516/354-1815

I Offer A Free ½ Hour Coaching Call

Rita Simon Fata, MBA, Professional Coach

I am the founder of *REACH & REALIZE COACHING SERVICES*, an organization formed to assist individuals and companies achieve success.

Whether you are seeking to improve your personal image, or enjoy greater career satisfaction, I can assist you in developing a systematic approach to master effective leadership and managerial skills. I can help you organize your personal thought processes to enable you to make prudent business decisions and achieve long-term professional goals. If you are contemplating a career change or returning to the workforce, let me show you how to apply your strengths to gain the confidence you will need to meet new and different challenges.

As a small business owner or entrepreneur, my formal education as an accountant and manager provides me with exceptional business acumen that enables me to help you develop results-oriented business and marketing plans to achieve success in your particular industry. Within the framework of a well thought out and progressive strategy, I will guide you, motivate you, and support you so that you stay focused and channel your energy efficiently and effectively.

After careful analysis and understanding of your aspirations and objectives, I am prepared to assist you in developing keynote presentations or interactive workshops to motivate your employees or engage and energize your audience or, if you prefer, I can provide these services to your organization, personally, on your behalf.

Are you an undergraduate trying to identify areas of special interest to find your path to success? Have you just completed your education and need help in channeling your skills and potential in the right direction? Or, are you ready to return to the workforce? We can discuss your special concerns or logistical matters such as updating your resume and presenting your time off in a positive light.

If you are working on your website, sales or marketing presentation, or any other business or academic writing, I can assist in editing and fine-tuning your written product so that it positively and creatively communicates your talents and expertise to its intended audience. Simple oversights in grammar, spelling, or punctuation can prevent you from moving to the next level of accomplishment. Don't allow this to happen.

Have you moved beyond your career? Are you looking forward to a rewarding retirement? I can assist you in discovering new interests and opportunities that will engage and energize your mind and spirit.

Open yourself to success. Take this opportunity to learn how to make the choices that will impact positively on you and your future happiness. Settle for nothing less than the best—you owe it to yourself!

Types of Clients I Work With:

- CEO's and CFO's; Human Resource, Sales, Marketing and Management Executives;
- Accounting, Legal, Health and Education Professionals; Small Business Owners; Entrepreneurs;
- Retirees; and all others seeking guidance in career or life matters.

Coaching Specialties:

- Executive and Business Coaching
- Leadership and Management Coaching
- Culture Creation; Communication Skills; Strategic Development; Conflict Resolution
- Career Coaching: Resume Preparation; Interviewing and Presentation Skills; Compensation Negotiation
- Career Change: Skills Assessment; Marketability Analysis; Networking Opportunities
- Editing/Writing (Website; Business; Academic)
- Image Consulting
- Retirement Planning
- Vocational Development
- Work-Life Balance

Professional Background:

For more than 20 years, I have worked with law firm owners directing the formulation of short and long-term budgets and determining spending criteria that directly affected business practices and positively impacted profitability; addressed all aspects of human resources, including recruiting, hiring, and developing key talent; created manuals concerning policies and procedures incorporating legal and ethical issues; implemented technological change in a precise and stable format; and developed all other programs to improve productivity by clearly defining goals and enhancing communication to achieve success.

I have experience in certain areas of the real estate industry, including management of rental property and specific construction projects, and creating and incorporating unique marketing techniques to promote occupancy and sales.

I have provided personal travel consulting services, offering custom and detailed itineraries for clients within the USA and abroad, with a particular emphasis on Europe, Africa. and India.

Working extensively with my husband, we have developed and promoted his company, Richard Fata Photography, which captures photographic images of people and places throughout the world with a special emphasis on wildlife and landscapes. This company also provides opportunities for like-minded individuals to enjoy thoughtful and imaginative workshops and journeys in local and distant environments.

Education:

Queens College of the City University of New York
BA, Accounting

Dowling College
MBA, Management

Contact Information:

Rita Simon Fata, MBA
Professional Coach
Telephone Number: 631-834-4300
Fax: 631-493-3417
E-mail: rita@reachandrealize.com
Web-site: www.reachandrealize.com

I offer a free ½ hr. introductory coaching appointment.

Siegmundo Hirsch, Ph.D., Personal and Career Coach

I am a personal and career coach. I lead workshops (at Hofstra University, New York Institute of Technology and Long Island University at CW Post College campus) on business-related subjects such as: management, conflict resolution, recruitment, retention, mid-life career reevaluation, interviewing, networking, communication (in English and Spanish), and cross-cultural understanding.

For over twenty years, I was a senior healthcare executive in charge of a diverse and multinational staff of hundreds. My experience encompasses administration, training and development of professional, managerial and non-exempt employees. I mentored and encouraged coworkers to further their education and reach for higher positions, whether in their current line or another field.

I assist my clients in identifying their interests, values and preferences, clarifying their aspirations, honing their leadership qualities, and strategizing to reach their goals. My focus is on customer satisfaction.
Personal characteristics include a quiet demeanor and strong resolve. I listen well and am friendly, flexible, and supportive.

Types of Clients I Work With:

I work with an international clientele, with people involved in career and other transitions, or who want to improve interpersonal relationships (whether at work or at home). I assist with goal clarification and achievement of purpose. My clients are individuals like you and me.

Former and present clients include business owners, public sector administrators, and employees of business, government and non-profit agencies.

Specialties:

- Small business owners and managers.
- Career changers and people in other transitions.
- Relationships.
- Immigrants learning about the ways and culture of the United States.
- Introverts.
- Fluency in Spanish and German.

Services:

- Coaching, in person, over the phone and by e-mail.
- Support with transitions.
- Career exploration.
- Assessment tools.
- Occupational research.
- Cover letters and other correspondence.
- Resume preparation.
- Job search training: interviewing, networking and negotiation.

Education and Professional Background:

- Ph.D. with a concentration in human resources.
- Completed post-graduate training in Gestalt therapy.
- MA in International Relations (with a concentration in Latin American politics) from New York University.
- BA in Government from The City College of New York.
- Certified in career counseling and development.
- Former CEO of nursing facilities in charge of a diverse staff of 300.
- Lead workshops at local universities on business-related subjects like interviewing, networking, cross-cultural understanding, management, conflict resolution.
- Fluent in Spanish and German. Teach Spanish and English as a second language.
- Writer for *Latin Long Island Magazine*.
- Author of *The Plight For Introverts*.

Memberships:

- International Coach Federation.
- International Association of Career Management Professionals
- Professional Resume Writing and Research Association
- Society for Human Resources Management
- Career Masters Institute (CMI)
- The (New York) Metropolitan Health Administrators' Association
- United Coaching Associates

Contact Information:

Contact: Siegmundo Hirsch, Ph.D., Personal & Professional Coach
Voice/Fax: 516-678-0619
E-mail: sh@career-coaching.com
Web-site: www.career-coaching.com

I Offer An Initial Consultation.

Bibliography

Baldwin, Christina. Life's Companion: Journal Writing as a Spiritual Quest. *Bantam Books, 1990 & 1991*

Beck, Martha, Finding Your Own North Star. Random House, New York, 2001

Bernd, Ed. Jose Silva's Ultramind ESP System. The Career Press Publishing Company, 2000.

Boldt, Laurence G. Zen and the Art of Making a Living: A Practical Guide to Creative Career Design. *Penguin/Arkana 1999, p.89*

Bolles, Richard N. What Color Is Your Parachute?—A Practical Manual for Job-Hunters & Career Changers. Ten Speed Press, Berkeley, CA, 2004

Breathnach, Sarah Ban, Simple Abundance, Warner Books, New York, 1995

Buckingham, Marcus, and Clifton, Donald O.. NOW, Discover your Strengths, The revolutionary program that shows you how to develop your unique talents and strengths—and those of the people you manage. Based on the Gallup study of over two million people. The Free Press, New York, 2001.

Canfield, Jack; Hansen, Mark Victor. The Aladdin Factor, Berkley Book, New York, 1995

Charvet, Shelle Rose. Words That Change Minds. Kendall/Hunt Publishing Company, 1997.

Chopra, MD, Deepak. The Seven Spiritual Laws of Success, Amber-Allen, San Rafael, CA 1994

Covey, Stephen. First Things First, Fireside, New York, 1994

Covey, Stephen. The 7 Habits of Highly Effective People, Fireside, New York 1989

DeAngelis, Barbara Are You The One For Me?. Dell Publishing, a division of Bantam Doubleday Dell Publishing Group, Inc., NY, 1993.

Department of Labor. Department of Labor's Occupational Outlook Handbook.

Dodd, Ray. The Power of Belief: Essential Tools for an Extraordinary Life. Mount Baldy Press, Inc., July 2004.

Dyer, Wayne D. You'll See It When You Believe It. HarperCollins, New York, 2001

Dyer, Wayne <u>The 10 Secrets for Success and Inner Peace</u>. Hay House, Carlsbad, CA 2001

Dyer, Wayne, W. <u>The Power Of Intentions</u>, Hay House, California, 2003

Farr, J. Michael. <u>The Complete Guide for Occupational Exploration: An Easy-To-Use Guide to Exploring over 12,000 Job Titles</u>. JIST Works, January 1, 1993

Farr, Michael J.; Shatkin, Lauren; Ludden, Laverne L. <u>Guide for Occupational Exploration</u>. JIST Works, Inc. 2001 Edition

Fiore, Neil <u>Overcoming Procrastination,</u>: MJF Books, New York 1989

Frankl, Viktor E. <u>Man's Search for Meaning</u>, Beacon Press, Boston, MA, 1992

Gawain, Shakti; <u>Creative Visualization</u>, New World Library, Novato, CA 1995

Grabhorn, Lynn. <u>Excuse Me Your Life is Waiting</u>. Hampton Roads Publishing Company, Inc., 2000.

Hay, Louise. <u>You Can Heal Your Life.</u> Hay House, Inc., CA, 1984.

Head, Simon. <u>The New Ruthless Economy: Work and Power in the Digital Age</u>. *(As quoted in the New York Times)* Oxford University Press, 2003

Jarow, Rick. <u>Creating the Work You Love: Courage, Commitment and Career</u>, *Destiny Books, 1995, p.24*

Jeffers, Susan. <u>Embracing Uncertainty</u>,St. Martin's Press, New York, 2004

Jist Publishing, 2004

Kushel, Gerald. <u>Effective Thinking For Uncommon Success</u>, AMACOM, New York, 1991

McGraw, Dr. Phil <u>Self Matters</u>, Simon & Schuster, New York, 2001

McGraw, Jay. <u>Life Strategies for Teens, A Fireside Book</u>. Simon&Shuster, 2000

McMeekin, Gail. <u>The 12 Secrets of Highly Creative Women</u>. Conari Press, Berkeley, CA 2000

Morgenstern, Julie. <u>Organizing from the Inside Out</u>: Henry Holt and Company, LLC, NY, 1998.

Morgenstern, Julie. <u>Time Management from the Inside Out</u>. Henry Holt and Company, LLC, NY, 2000.

O'Hanlon, Bill. <u>Do One Thing Different</u>, Quill, New York, 1999

Paul, Ph.D, Marilyn. <u>It's Hard to Make a Difference When You Can't Find Your Keys</u>. Viking Compass, a member of Penguin Putnam Inc., NY, 2003.

Platkin, Charles, Stuart. <u>Breaking The Pattern</u>, Red Mill Press, New York, 2002

Prather, Hugh. The Little Book of Letting Go, Conari Press, Boston, MA 2000

Resources/Recommendations: www.SilvaUltraMind.net, www.LynnGrabhorn.com and www.shellerosecharvet.com

Richardson, Cheryl. Life Makeovers Broadway Books, New York, 2000

Richardson, Cheryl. Take Time for Your Life Random House, New York, 1999

Robbins, Anthony. Unlimited Power, Free Press, New York 1986

Ruiz, Don Miguel. The Four Agreements: A Practical Guide to Personal Freedom. Amber-Allen Publishing, November 1, 1997.

Sheehy, Gail Passages, Bantam, New York, 1976

Sher, Barbara, I Could Do Anything if I Only Knew What it Was. Dell, New York, 1994

Siegel, MD, Bernie. Prescriptions for Living, Quill, New York, 1998

Thomas, Katherine Woodward. Calling In "The One"; 7 Weeks to Attract the Love of Your Life. Three Rivers Press, NY, 2004.

Tolle, Eckhart. The Power of Now. New World Library, Novato, CA, 1999

Tracy, Brian. Eat That Frog! 21 Great Ways to Stop Procrastinating and Get More Done in Less Time. Berrett-Koehler Publishers, 2002.

Weider, Marcia. Making Your Dreams Come True, Finding Your Passion With America's Dream Coach. Harmony Books, New York, 1999.

Zukav, Gary. The Seat of the Soul, Fireside, New York 1989

0-595-33048-7